The Greased Cartridge

E. Jaiwant Paul is a man of varied interests, having authored eight other books, including *Rani of Jhansi*, *The Story of Tea*, *Baji Rao*, *The Unforgettable Maharajas*, *Har Dayal: The Great Revolutionary* (co-author Mrs Shubh Paul), *Arms and Armour: Traditional Weapons of India*, and *Annals and Antiquities of Rajasthan*. He is on the expert panel on weapons for several museums of Rajasthan.

A hardcore corporate, he initially worked for Hindustan Unilever and was later Director of Brooke Bond, India. Thereafter he headed the National Mineral Water Company in Muscat, Oman. A keen cricketer and tennis player, he now lives in Delhi and serves as director of a few companies.

OTHER TITLES BY E. JAIWANT PAUL

Rani of Jhansi,
The Story of Tea
Baji Rao
The Unforgettable Maharajas
Har Dayal: The Great Revolutionary
Arms and Armour: Traditional Weapons of India
Annals and Antiquities of Rajasthan

OTHER LOTUS TITLES

Ajit Bhattacharjea	*Sheikh Mohammad Abdullah: Tragic Hero of Kashmir*
Amarinder Singh	*The Last Sunset: The Rise and Fall of the Lahore Durbar*
Anil Dharker	*Icons: Men & Women Who Shaped Today's India*
Aitzaz Ahsan	*The Indus Saga: The Making of Pakistan*
Alam Srinivas & TR Vivek	*IPL: The Inside Story*
Amir Mir	*The True Face of Jehadis: Inside Pakistan's Terror Networks*
Ashok Mitra	*The Starkness of It*
Dr Humanyun Khan & G. Parthasarthy	*Diplomatic Divide*
Gyanendra Pandey & Yunus Samad	*Faultlines of Nationhood*
H.L.O. Garrett	*The Trial of Bahadur Shah Zafar*
M.J. Akbar	*India: The Siege Within*
M.J. Akbar	*Kashmir: Behind the Vale*
M.J. Akbar	*The Shade of Swords*
M.J. Akbar	*Byline*
M.J. Akbar	*Blood Brothers: A Family Saga*
Maj. Gen. Ian Cardozo	*Param Vir: Our Heroes in Battle*
Maj. Gen. Ian Cardozo	*The Sinking of INS Khukri: What Happened in 1971*
Madhu Trehan	*Tehelka as Metaphor*
Mushirul Hasan	*India Partitioned. 2 Vols*
Mushirul Hasan	*John Company to the Republic*
Mushirul Hasan	*Knowledge, Power and Politics*
Nayantara Sahgal (ed.)	*Before Freedom: Nehru's Letters to His Sister*
Nilima Lambah	*A Life Across Three Continents*
Robert Hutchison	*The Raja of Harsil: The Legend of Frederick 'Pahari' Wilson*
Sharmishta Gooptu and Boria Majumdar (eds)	*Revisiting 1857: Myth, Memory, History*
Shashi Joshi	*The Last Durbar*
Shashi Tharoor & Shaharyar M. Khan	*Shadows across the Playing Field*
Shrabani Basu	*Spy Princess: The Life of Noor Inayat Khan*
Shyam Bhatia	*Goodbye Shahzadi: A Political Biography*
Thomas Weber	*Gandhi, Gandhism and the Gandhians*
Thomas Weber	*Going Native: Gandhi's Relationship with Western Women*

FORTHCOMING TITLES

CNN-IBN	*Real Heroes: Ordinary People Extraordinary Service*
Mohammed Hyder	*October Coup: A Memoir of the Struggle for Hyderabad*

The Greased Cartridge

THE HEROES AND VILLAINS OF 1857-58

E. Jaiwant Paul

LOTUS COLLECTION
ROLI BOOKS

The Lotus Collection
An imprint of
Roli Books Pvt Ltd
M-75, Greater Kailash II Market
New Delhi 110 048
Phone: ++91 (011) 4068 2000
Fax: ++91 (011) 2921 7185
E-mail: info@rolibooks.com; Website: www.rolibooks.com

Also at
Bangalore, Chennai & Mumbai

Cover: Kanchon Mitra

ISBN: 978-81-7436-823-2

Typeset in Adobe Caslon Pro by Roli Books Pvt Ltd
and printed at Sanat Printers, Haryana.

CONTENTS

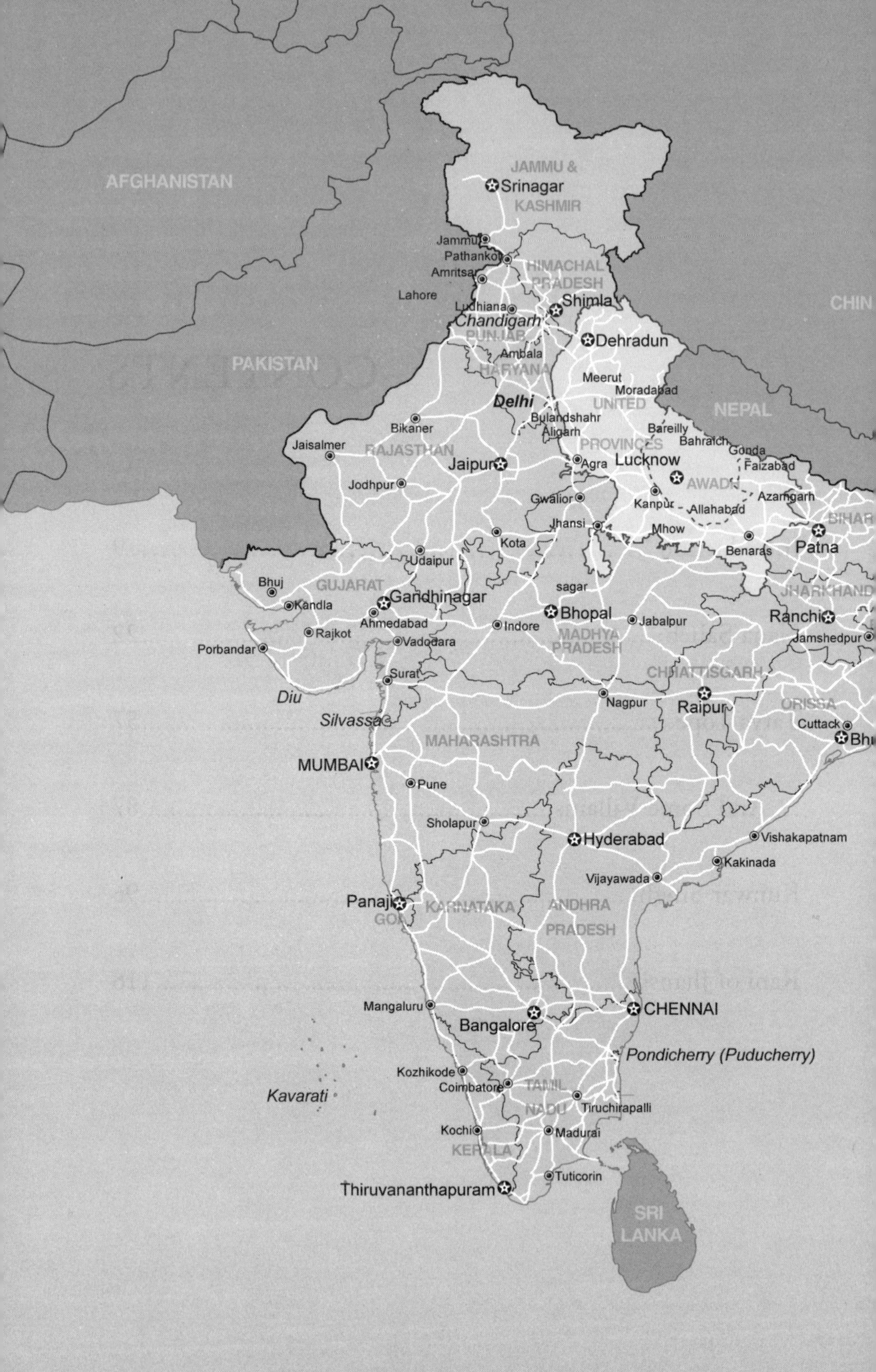

AFGHANISTAN
PAKISTAN
NEPAL
SRI LANKA
JAMMU &
KASHMIR
Srinagar
Jammu
Pathankot
Amritsar
Lahore
HIMACHAL
PRADESH
Shimla
Ludhiana
Chandigarh
PUNJAB
Dehradun
Ambala
HARYANA
Delhi
Meerut
Moradabad
UNITED
PROVINCES
Bulandshahr
Aligarh
Bareilly
Bahraich
Gonda
Faizabad
Lucknow
AWADH
Agra
Kanpur
Allahabad
Azamgarh
Gwalior
Jhansi
Mhow
Benaras
BIHAR
Patna
JHARKHAND
Ranchi
Jamshedpur
Bikaner
Jaisalmer
RAJASTHAN
Jaipur
Jodhpur
Kota
Udaipur
Bhuj
GUJARAT
Kandla
Gandhinagar
Ahmedabad
Rajkot
Porbandar
Vadodara
Surat
Diu
Silvassa
sagar
Bhopal
Indore
Jabalpur
MADHYA
PRADESH
CHHATTISGARH
Raipur
Nagpur
ORISSA
Cuttack
MAHARASHTRA
MUMBAI
Pune
Sholapur
Hyderabad
Vishakapatnam
Kakinada
Vijayawada
Panaji
KARNATAKA
ANDHRA
PRADESH
Mangaluru
Bangalore
CHENNAI
Pondicherry (Puducherry)
Kozhikode
Coimbatore
TAMIL
NADU
Tiruchirapalli
Kavarati
Kochi
Madurai
KERALA
Tuticorin
Thiruvananthapuram

Storm Centres

- Barrackpore
- Meerut
- Delhi
- Lucknow
- Kanpur
- Jhansi
- Jagdishpur

Dedicated to

Shubh, Nisha, Viveka, Karan and Subroto

INTRODUCTION

It is not often realized that the Revolt of 1857-58 was the biggest and bloodiest conflict against any European colonial power during the nineteenth century. It involved over two hundred thousand soldiers on both sides, as well as innumerable Indian civilians and peasants who picked up their *talwar*s and muskets and fought the British. The fighting went on for almost two years and mutual hatred led to unbelievable atrocities.

This story is essentially about the heroes – Tatya Tope, Nana Saheb, Rani Lakshmi Bai of Jhansi, Kunwar Singh of Jagdishpur – and not to forget, a few villains. As the great revolt forms the backdrop to their stories, let's start with a brief account of it.

It started as a one-man rebellion on 29 March 1857. Lieutenant B.H. Baugh arrived at the lines in Barrackpore near Kolkata, and saw a single *sipahi* (anglicized to 'sepoy') marching up and down in front of the guard comprising twenty men, exhorting them to join him and strike a blow for their religion. 'Come out you *behnchud*s (seducers of sisters) why are you not joining me? You are the ones who incited me to do this. Get ready you *behnchud*s.' The *sipahi* also threatened to shoot the first white man he saw. It was no idle threat, for as soon as the *sipahi* saw Lt Baugh, he fired. The shot missed Baugh but brought his horse down. The lieutenant also fired, but missed. Then began a desperate hand-to-hand encounter. The *sipahi* drew his *talwar*, there was an arcing flash of steel and Baugh was desperately clutching his bloodied arm. Sergeant-Major James Thornton Hewson rushed to his help, but the *sipahi* was a better swordsman than either of them and wounded not only Baugh but also the sergeant. The guard of twenty *sipahi*s stood stock still and watched the *firanghee*s (foreigners) fighting for their lives. The sergeant shouted for help; only one man from the guard, Sheikh Paltu came forward. He crept up behind the fighting *sipahi* and held him from the back. The two white soldiers ran for their lives. The *sipahi* then taunted his comrades for letting him fight alone. Meanwhile, other European officers rushed to the scene. Brigadier Grant drew his revolver and told the guard, 'The first man who refuses to obey the order is a dead man.' Sullenly the guard moved forward. When the lone rebel saw the day was lost, he turned the musket upon himself. He was wounded but unfortunately could not save himself from a felon's death. The *sipahi*, Mangal Pandey, was twenty-six years old. Soon, the cry 'Remember Mangal Pandey' was to become a signal of revolt.

The Mutiny, the Great Revolt or Rebellion, the National Uprising or the War of Independence – call it what you will, scholars are still arguing about it. By 1857, the strength of white soldiers in India had fallen to 45,000. The rest had been dispatched by the British government to Crimea and Persia. Indian *sipahi*s of the Bengal army who rebelled numbered about 100,000. Two-thirds of the Bengal army was made up of 'Purabia' Hindus from the area around Avadh. It contained 35 per cent Rajputs, 31 per cent Brahmins, and 15 per cent Muslims, while low-caste Hindus and others formed the rest. The dominance of the upper caste becomes an important factor, as we see later.

It is also relevant to note that Hindus and Muslims fought as one during the revolt. Their common aim was to liberate themselves from the British yoke. This feeling of unity was found not only in the army, but also in the civil population. Hindus and Muslims had developed friendly relations as a result of sharing centuries of common life. It was after the 1857 revolt that the British thought it was important to breach this unity. Steps were then taken by them so that common action by the two communities would be impossible in the future.

Maharaja Scindia of Gwalior, the Nizam of Hyderabad, and the states of the Punjab, the Sikh sipahis as well as some Punjabi Muslims and Pathans came to the assistance of the beleaguered British. The

Sikhs in particular, long hostile to Mughal rule and lately worsted by the now mutinous 'Purabias' of the Bengal army, promptly gravitated to the British. The Raja of Jind even offered to personally lead his troops against the rebels. Had it not been for them, the story of 1857-58 might well have been different.

George Bruce Malleson, a noted historian of the mutiny, says, 'For four months, Scindia had probably the fate of India in his hands. Had he revolted in June, the siege of Delhi must have been raised; Agra and Lucknow would have fallen. It is more than probable that the Punjab would have risen.' Innes, another historian, says, 'Scindia's loyalty saved India for the British.' Thomas Rice Holmes, well known for his history of the mutiny, has described Salar Jung, the minister of Hyderabad as 'a man whose name deserves to be ever mentioned by Englishmen with gratitude and admiration.'

In addition to the above, the Begum of Bhopal, Gulab Singh of Kashmir, the Maharaja of Jodhpur, and importantly, Jang Bahadur of Nepal, with a strong Gurkha army, rendered invaluable help to the British enemy. The people mentioned in the last few paragraphs consigned us to ninety years more of slavery.

Interestingly, while the Maharaja of Gwalior stuck with the British, his well-trained army joined Tatya Tope and the Rani of Jhansi and fought against the imperialists at a later stage. In the case of Jodhpur too, while the Maharaja immediately offered to help his masters, the Jodhpur legion deserted to the rebels.

The areas south of the Narmada river did not join the revolt. The armies of the Madras and Bombay presidencies remained loyal to their foreign masters and helped restore order at a later stage.

Avadh was the main recruiting ground of the 'Purabias' for the Bengal army. It had also been recently and most unjustifiably annexed by the British. In Avadh and several other areas of Uttar Pradesh, the landed aristocracy and *talukdar*s had been deprived of their lands. There was a traditional bond between them and their retainers and peasants. Thus when the revolt broke out, the rural population swelled the ranks of the rebels and Avadh became the main arena of war. Indeed, here it was clearly a national uprising with armed civilians outnumbering the mutineers in the insurrection.

The causes of the uprising have been discussed in depth by academicians. Here I will only mention that there were a host of social, economic, religious, and political grievances, tangible and intangible, responsible for the revolt. Lord Dalhousie's 'Doctrine of Lapse' had enabled Britain to acquire several states, including Jhansi, by legal stratagem and this led to deep hostility, not only among the ruling princes, but also the people. The unscrupulous annexation of Avadh has already been mentioned.

India's economic history shows that it was an exporter of fine textiles and luxury goods. The British demolished Indian industry and from being an exporter of high-quality products, it became an exporter of raw materials. Between 1820 and 1840, this de-industrialization closed down thousands of units operated by peasants and small entrepreneurs. The peasant element, thus driven to penury, joined in the revolt and gave it a much wider base.

A fact we have highlighted earlier is the dominant proportion of high-caste Hindus in the army. This section was appalled by widespread rumours that the British were determined to convert them to Christianity. The abolition of *sati* and the encouragement of widow remarriage, along with the aggressive activities of missionaries, convinced the sipahis of their secret plans to destroy the religion of the country.

In most accounts of the revolt, the greased cartridge has been referred to as the spark and tinder that lit the flames of rebellion. Benjamin Disraeli said in parliament, 'Revolutions are not made of grease,' implying that there were many other underlying causes. The greased cartridge – what was it all about? The army so far had been equipped with the smooth-barrelled musket, which had a protracted loading procedure and was not accurate over long ranges. The new Enfield rifles, which were now being issued, had grooved or rifled barrels. This made them more accurate and gave them a longer range. The powder and bullet for the new rifle were put together in a paper cartridge. To load the rifle, the end of the cartridge containing the powder had to be bitten off so that the charge would ignite. The cartridge was then rammed down the muzzle of the rifle. To make the ramming easier, the cartridge was heavily greased. The grease used was tallow, probably containing both cow and pig fat. To 'the cow reverencing Hindu and the pig paranoid Muslims' having to bite this was repellent, defiling and deadly to their religious prospects.

The sipahis refused to touch the new rifles. What was more dangerous for the British were rumours that, apart from the cartridges, they were mixing the crushed bones of cows and pigs into flour and sugar as part of a conspiracy to convert the sipahis to Christianity. This caused much rancour and as the rumours spread, they were often magnified and distorted.

A sidelight was the appearance of the mysterious *chapattis*. It was reported that four *chapattis* would be sent to the watchmen of four villages and each village in turn had been told to send four more *chapattis* to four other villages and so on. Thus, the distribution of *chapattis* increased in geometric progression. By this means, the *chapattis* were travelling all over Hindustan at the rate of 150 kilometres in twenty-four hours. Newspapers in Delhi were full of this phenomenon. It was also being said that an ominous slogan '*Sub lal hogai hai*' (Everything is becoming red), was being whispered everywhere. However, the exact significance of these curious *chapattis* was never understood. Many thought they signalled that dramatic upheavals were about to take place across Hindustan. It was also said that upon the downfall of the Maratha power, a piece of bread had passed from village to village. Thus it was now signalling the collapse of British power.

Although it all started with the one-man rebellion of Mangal Pandey, he was almost irrelevant to the mutiny. The actual revolt started almost a month and a half later at Meerut, an important military station. Eighty-five sipahis, revulsed at the idea of biting the greased cartridges, refused to do so and were court marshalled. The commander at Meerut was sixty-seven-years-old General W. Hewitt. He was extremely fat and absolutely lazy. A colleague described him as 'a fearful old dolt … An exasperating idiot.' Hewitt rejected a plea for mercy against the ten years rigorous imprisonment imposed on these eighty-five men who had refused to bite the cartridges, and even suggested the death sentence for some of them.

The sentenced sipahis were assembled in front of the cantonment troops, white soldiers with their guns loaded and sabres drawn. The sipahis, some with several years of honourable service behind them, were stripped of their uniforms, their boots removed and their ankles shackled. When they were marched off, they threw their boots at the colonel and cursed loudly in Hindustani, '*In lal moo ke bandroon se badla!*' (Revenge against these red-faced monkeys!) These were proud men who had fought for the British in many campaigns and never wavered in their allegiance.

A day after the public humiliation of these brave soldiers, on 10 May 1857, their comrades in arms at Meerut rose as one to free them. They broke open the armoury and rampaged through the cantonment, massacred Europeans and set their bungalows on fire. Interestingly, there were as many British as Indian troops in the station, and more importantly, the British had artillery, yet no resistance was organized by them. Military authorities were paralysed. Even stranger was that British intelligence was so poor that it had no idea of the coming catastrophe. While the weather permitted, cricket matches were being lost and won, and in the cantonment, the ritual of balls and racing was being enjoyed.

Having slaughtered most of the foreigners in sight, the sipahis rode the 100 kilometres to Delhi, galloped across the bridge of boats that spanned the Yamuna and entered the capital. The sipahis from Delhi cantonment also joined them and, while the city resounded to their war cry, '*Deen, Deen,*' (faith) they put all foreigners to the sword. They then went to the Red Fort and called upon Bahadur Shah Zafar to assume command. He was eighty-two years old and had been on the throne for twenty years, but he was a king without a kingdom, 'a chess-board king'. Although he was still revered by the man in the street as the lineal successor of Akbar and Shah Jahan, he was a puppet of the British and his authority lay within the confines of the Red Fort. The sipahis galloped into the open-air audience hall of the fort with swords drawn and demanded that he take over as the rightful emperor. Bahadur Shah pleaded old age and infirmity, he pleaded poverty, but the rebels would not be denied. They had come to resurrect the Mughal Empire and fight for both

Hinduism and Islam. And so this broken old man was hailed as the Emperor of Hindustan. The proclamation was accompanied by booming cannons and the news went around that the British Raj had ended.

The co-option of the Mughals transformed the insurgency. A regimental mutiny had acquired the character of a political revolt whose legitimacy transcended that of the British regime. The mutineers were thus seen as liberators and warriors fighting an enemy government and restoring the old order, of which the King of Delhi was the rightful representative. This consequently invited a host of civilian adherents.

The loss of Delhi was a severe blow to British prestige. The Punjab remained peaceful, mainly because the *Purabia* sipahis posted there were immediately disarmed, while the Sikhs and Punjabi Muslims remained loyal to their foreign masters. News of the uprising travelled at an astonishing speed, mainly by word of mouth and rebellions broke out over a vast area covering the Indo-Gangetic plain, central India and parts of Rajasthan. On 30 May 1857, the sipahis rose in Lucknow, and British residents led by Henry Lawrence had to take refuge in the residency. The very next day, the sipahis rebelled at Bareilly, under the leadership of Subedar Bakht Khan, who was later appointed by Bahadur Shah as the chief of the rebel forces at Delhi. In the next few days, uprisings started at Kanpur, Allahabad, and Jhansi. At Kanpur, the leadership of the rebels was assumed by Nana Dhondu Pant, popularly called Nana Saheb, the adopted son of the ex-Peshwa, Baji Rao II. He established his government there and was assisted by his friends and advisors Tatya Tope and Azimullah Khan. In Avadh, Begum Hazrat Mahal, the wife of the ex-king, led the revolt. The more prominent leader of the revolt here was however Ahmadullah Shah, the maulvi of Faizabad. Rani Lakshmibai, the young widow of the maharaja, took control in Jhansi and personally led her troops in battle against the British. In Bihar, the formidable Rajput chieftain Kunwar Singh, all of eighty years of age, won remarkable victories against the British and gave them no respite for eighteen months.

Civilians and peasants soon joined the rebel sipahis. Gujjars, a semi-nomadic pastoral tribe from around Delhi and Rajasthan, became active in looting British cantonments. Other plunderers joined in and anarchy spread throughout the country.

All these revolts in various parts of the country generally followed the pattern of Meerut. The sipahis killed European officers, in many cases sparing neither women nor children. They released prisoners from jails, plundered territories, burnt government offices, and either set off for Delhi or joined some local chieftain. Hatred was mutual and horrendous atrocities were committed by both sides. This is an aspect that we shall cover later.

Suppression of the Revolt

It took the British almost two years to put down the revolt. They summoned reinforcements from the Madras army, called in Highlanders from the Persian expedition, and diverted British regiments on their way to China, to protect and encourage the murderous drug trade that the British were forcing on the Chinese people, to India. More troops also arrived from England and, as there was no Suez Canal, they crossed the isthmus overland, on foot.

All this was done in such panic-stricken haste that in the intense summer heat of 1858, with temperatures soaring above 44°C, these troops fought in heavy woollen uniforms and even brass helmets, which troopers claimed became so hot that you could toast bread inside them. No wonder that 8,000 of the entrants died of sunstroke. It is interesting to note that Tatya Tope, in his various battles, carried out his main attacks at midday, when the heat was at its most intense and the powerful sun did as much as the rebel's musketry fire.

However, the disparity in numbers, which hampered the British in the early months, was overcome. The additional troops were augmented by their Indian auxiliaries, chiefly the Sikhs, Punjabi Muslims, Gurkhas and the armies of some of the princely states. Despite this, however, eight months more of fighting lay ahead.

In this chapter, we deal more with the revolt in Delhi and less with the happenings in Lucknow, Kanpur, and Jhansi, because events in the latter three centres are covered in detail later.

The recovery of Delhi was of supreme importance for the British. With the help of reinforcements, they defeated the rebels at Badli Ki Sarai, which is near the capital and occupied the Delhi ridge. They were restricted here for the next three months while twenty actions were fought in the vicinity. The Anglophile rajas of the Punjab, particularly the Raja of Jind, kept the British on the ridge supplied with food and other amenities.

Brigadier John Nicholson arrived in Delhi from the Punjab, followed by a seige train of heavy artillery and explosives that was enough to grind Delhi to dust. The assault began on 14 September 1857 at Kashmiri Gate, which is not far from the ridge. Much has been written about Nicholson, who led the assault, and has been hailed as the 'Hero of Delhi'. He had fought in the Sikh and Afghan wars. Within a few hours of the start of the battle, Nicholson was shot dead. His role in the actual fighting, therefore, was very limited.

The city was strongly defended and the battle raged for six days. The rebels fought with raw courage. At one stage, they even found an unexpected ally in alcohol. On the night of 15 September, British and Sikh soldiers found large quantities of brandy, beer and arrack in the city cellars and temporarily fell out of the battle, dead drunk! General Archdale Wilson then ordered that every remaining bottle was to be destroyed. However, the rebels were handicapped by their old-fashioned smooth-bore muskets, which were no match for the longer-ranged and more accurate Enfield rifles, now being used by British units. Houses in the city had been loop-holed by the sipahis and there was fierce house-to-house fighting. The sipahis were finally defeated, but at the cost of high casualties for the British. By 21 September, the British had occupied the Red Fort.

After the Red Fort had been captured, the British went looking for Bahadur Shah. He had taken refuge in the shadow of the tomb of his ancestor Humayun. The emperor surrendered to Captain William Hodson, who promptly and personally shot dead his three sons, although they had freely given up their arms. The following day, Hodson wrote to his sister, 'In twenty-four hours, I disposed of the principal members of the house of Timur the Tartar … I confess I did enjoy the opportunity of ridding the earth of these wretches.' Their corpses were put on public display and all Europeans in Delhi congratulated Hodson saying, 'We hope you will bag many more.'

The fall of Delhi was a catastrophe for the rebels. The British soldiers 'maddened by a heady mixture of fatigue, liquor and bloody rumour turned violently on the city and its inhabitants'. Delhi then suffered its reign of terror. There was no sanctity of life or property. The innocent suffered along with the rebels; they were shot and strung up on gibbets; the revenge was bloody and cruel. The British plundered everything and everyone in sight. Houses were stripped and enormous treasure unearthed. This was followed by the British Prize Agents, who were no less rapacious. The reign of terror in Delhi continued for five months till February 1858. Ghalib, the great poet wrote, 'Here is a vast ocean of blood before me. God alone knows what more I have to behold … Thousands of my friends are dead, who should I remember and to whom should I complain? Perhaps none is left even to shed tears on my grave.' Bahadur Shah became a prisoner. He was tried and banished to Yangon (Rangoon), where he died a few years later, far from his home and his family, unhonoured and unsung. His grave, which I visited on a recent visit, is located in the centre of Yangon. It is a simple grave with no embellishment and is under a shed-like structure, surrounded by a small garden.

Besides Delhi, the war was fought on two other fronts, Kanpur and Lucknow in United Provinces and Jhansi in central India. The rebellion spread with astonishing speed. Despite the large reinforcements received by the British from the Punjab and the large number of troops brought in from South Africa and England, its suppression proved difficult.

General Henry Havelock was sent with fresh troops to restore authority at Kanpur and Lucknow. His advance on Kanpur (or Cawnpore as the English called it) was fiercely contested by Nana Saheb and the Indian sipahis, but superior equipment and better leadership enabled him to enter Kanpur on 17 July 1857. Nana Saheb evacuated the place and escaped to Avadh. Havelock then crossed the Ganges for the relief of Lucknow. He was opposed at every step and had to retreat twice. It was only three months later that he was able to reach the Residency at Lucknow. However, he could do little to help the besieged British and merely added his troops to the encircled garrison. The siege of Lucknow by the rebel forces continued and they were augmented by numerous retainers of the Avadh *talukdar*s who had joined the struggle.

Sir Colin Campbell, who was the commander-in-chief, next arrived at Kanpur with a strong contingent on 3 November 1857. He was joined by troops that could now be spared from Delhi. After hard fighting, he reached Lucknow, but he encountered such strong resistance from the rebels there that he had to fall back to Kanpur. On his return he found that the city had been occupied by Tatya Tope, who had defeated General Windham in a battle there. However, on Campbell's return, Tatya Tope could not retain his hold on the city and had to withdraw.

Four months later, Campbell moved again from Kanpur to Lucknow and this time he was able to regain it. The rebels, however, continued to fight in the area but then the Gurkhas arrived in strength from Nepal and their help to the British was crucial. Begum Hazrat Mahal and her numerous followers in Avadh were able to make their escape to Nepal, as did Nana and his troops.

In Bihar, the most formidable challenge to British authority came from Kunwar Singh, the eighty-year-old doughty Rajput chieftain of Jagdishpur in Shahabad district. He assumed command of the sipahis, who had revolted at Danapur on 25 July 1857. Two days later, he occupied Arrah, the district headquarters. Captain Dunbar, sent to recapture Arrah, was killed and his troops ignominiously beaten by Kunwar Singh. Later, however, Vincent Eyre defeated Kunwar Singh; recaptured Arrah; and destroyed his ancestral seat, Jagdishpur. Kunwar Singh then entered Uttar Pradesh and, in March 1858, occupied Azamgarh, for which he had been granted a *farman* by the King of Avadh. He was, however, attacked by a British force and had to leave the place and retreat towards Bihar. In April 1858, Kunwar Singh won a signal victory near Jagdishpur against a British force led by Captain Le Grand. But soon after, the old warrior died of wounds suffered in his last battle.

In central India, Tatya Tope carried on a desperate struggle. He joined forces with the Rani of Jhansi, who, after a heroic resistance against a strong British force led by Sir Hugh Rose, had to give up her seat of government. Both Tatya Tope and the Rani fought two further battles at Kunch and Kalpi but were defeated. In sore straits and surrounded by enemy forces they acted with great daring and captured the city and fortress of Gwalior, forcing the maharaja, who was a great British ally, to flee. In these two battles, the Rani personally led cavalry charges right up to the mouth of the enemy's cannons.

In June 1858, British forces attacked Gwalior and in this battle Rani Lakshmi Bai was killed. Tatya Tope escaped and, having only limited resources, he resorted to guerilla warfare and baffled British commanders for almost one year. His aim was to fight his way to Maharashtra and engineer an uprising there, but he was betrayed by an ally and captured. After a hurried trial, he was hanged.

The struggle was marked by merciless killing and many innocent men, women and children were slaughtered on both sides. The British swore vengeance when they heard of the excesses committed by the sipahis at Meerut and Delhi. Similarly, the two massacres at Kanpur committed by Indians were the direct result of the inhuman acts of the British at Benaras and Allahabad.

In Allahabad, Colonel James Neill bombarded the town and set large areas on fire. As the inhabitants tried to escape the fire, they were shot down by grapeshot from cannons. Neill was promoted to the rank of General but, soon after, was ambushed by sipahis in the streets of Lucknow and shot through the head.

While British historians have described the atrocities of Indians in grisly detail, they have, with a few honourable exceptions, glossed over the horrors perpetuated by their own countrymen. Throwing away their mask of civilization, the British engaged in such savagery that, as one English writer put it, 'a reasonable parallel can be seen in our own times with the Nazi occupation of Europe'.

All Englishmen were not in favour of such cruel treatment and many raised their voices in protest. Lord Canning, the governor general, genuinely tried to put an end to this madness and, for this, his countrymen nicknamed him in derision, 'Clemency Canning'.

The revolt failed in its objective. But 'even in failure the Revolt of 1857 served a grand purpose. A source of inspiration for the national liberation movement, which later achieved what the Revolt could not.'

NANA SAHEB

Nana Saheb was a very controversial figure of the revolt. Many historians have labelled him a treacherous villain, while others have exonerated him from this charge and regard him as a rebel leader of consequence.

Nana's father, Baji Rao II, the last Peshwa, was defeated by the British in 1818 in the Third Anglo-Maratha war. He was deposed and had to leave Pune, the seat of his government. He was granted a pension and exiled from his former dominion. An alternate home had to be found for him. Initially, the British thought that Varanasi would be the best place, but on consideration they felt several factors could make this dangerous. Baji Rao was the erstwhile head of the most powerful empire in India. Varanasi was the holiest place of Hindu pilgrimage and several exiled princes were already living there. This could result in conspiracy and mischief. The British then offered Monghyr and Gorakhpur, but the Peshwa objected 'as the heat of Monghyr would kill him' and Gorakhpur had no temples of sanctity. Baji Rao would have preferred Mathura, but that was too close to the British frontier at the time. The official choice then fell on Bithur, about 10 kilometres from Kanpur. Baji Rao thus lived in Bithur for the next thirty years.

Bithur today is a half-forgotten village surrounded by brilliant yellow mustard fields. There are, however, the remains of the Peshwa's palace and several temples dating from the eighteenth century. The broad shining Ganges flows by. The temples have no worshippers and priests, and when evening comes, there is hardly a ray of light in any of them. But Bithur had seen better days before the British destroyed it in 1858.

A pension of eight lakh rupees per annum was granted to Baji Rao for 'the support of himself and his family'. Land was also granted to him as *jagir* and this was placed outside the jurisdiction of civil and criminal courts. Baji Rao settled here with about 1,200 retainers. He was a popular and respected figure in his retirement, not only due to his charities, but also the curious interest people attach to fallen greatness. Many never ceased to regard him as the Peshwa. After all, his Maratha predecessors were the dominant power and had challenged the British for supremacy in India.

Baji Rao did not disappear from the political scene and remained a source of anxiety to the British. There were rumours that he was intriguing with the Nepalese government, and more serious insinuations that he was hatching a conspiracy with Burma and Tibet.

It was understood that Baji Rao's pension would cease with his death. The British thought that as he was not in good health, this liability would not be a long-term one. Baji Rao belied all such expectations and, in the tranquil and carefree environs of Bithur, he lived till the ripe old age of seventy-seven and died only six years before the outbreak of the revolt.

Despairing of having a son and heir, the ex-Peshwa adopted three sons: Dhondu Pant, better known as Nana Saheb, Sadashiv Pant, and Gangadhar Rao. He also left two minor daughters and a grand-nephew, who were recognized as his dependents. Sadashiv Rao, the second son, predeceased his father.

In his will written in 1839, Baji Rao left his title and estates to the eldest of his adopted sons, Nana Saheb, who it was mentioned 'would be master and heir to the *gaddi* (throne) of the Peshwa'.

The eight-lakh-rupee pension granted by the East India Company was to cease with his death. Baji Rao was anxious to have some provision for his family and made efforts that a part of this pension be continued to his successor. Over the years, he made several requests to the governor general, as well as the directors of the East India Company that 'some provision be made for his adopted son

Nana, who would be the sole possessor of his wealth and property'. This wrangling with British authorities over the pension went on for several years and the issue was not allowed to rest. The position at the time of death was that Nana's claim was 'restricted to the private property of the Peshwa only'.

Although Nana Saheb was one of the major leaders of the Revolt, not much is known about his early life and training. This is not altogether surprising, because terror stalked the country after the Revolt, and no Indian dared write freely about the events. At the time of his father's death, Nana was in his mid-thirties and from the comments of various English soldiers, bureaucrats and writers, one gets some sort of a picture of the man.

Nana Saheb apparently made a favourable impression on Morland, who was the commissioner of the region. He described Nana as a 'quiet unostentatious young man and not at all addicted to any extravagant habits'. John Lang, who enjoyed Nana's hospitality for a few days, regarded him as a mediocrity. In his *Wanderings in India,* John Lang says, 'He appeared to me not a man of ability, nor a fool. He was selfish, but what native is not? He seemed to be far from a bigot in matters of religion.'

Private Henry Metcalf saw him drive to church. 'It is scarcely to be believed,' writes Metcalf, 'that Nana accompanied the Regiment to Church on the Sunday before we left Cawnpore. I saw him myself riding in a beautiful phaeton, drawn by two splendid grey horses.'

Nana's English doctor thought he was 'an excessively uninteresting person'. Colonel Mande states that 'Nana was between thirty and forty years of age, of middle height, stolid features and increasing stoutness.' He was supposed to be extremely fond of food and of dancing girls with 'eyes rubbed round with lamp black and sensual lips rosy with the juice of betel nut'.

From Indian sources, one learns that Nana was educated, and apart from Hindi and Marathi, he had some knowledge of Sanskrit. Nana and Tatya Tope were together as young boys at Bithur and were educated together. Lakshmi Bai, who later became the Rani of Jhansi, also lived in Bithur, and although much younger than the boys, she joined them regularly at their lessons. Interestingly, the three fought the British, either separately or jointly, in the Revolt of 1857.

Despite the education he received, Nana's knowledge of English was very rudimentary and he could not speak it well. English language newspapers, including the *Delhi Gazette* and the *Englishman,* were delivered to his palace but he employed a Eurasian to explain their contents to him.

Nana lived the life of an Indian prince. His palace was luxurious and decorated with finely-designed mirrors in which were reflected the sparkling chandeliers. Persian and Kashmiri carpets covered the floors. He is also reported to have had a gallery of pictures 'horribly unfit for any human eye,' painted by both European and Indian artists. His wardrobe was lavish and on special occasions he would appear wearing pearl and diamond necklaces and girt with his father's sword of state, which had a diamond-studded hilt and was embellished in gold damascene. He had a splendid collection of swords, daggers and armour from all ages, as well guns by celebrated European makers. He had laid out a beautiful garden around his palace. He was fond of animals and maintained a large menagerie, which included an astonishing variety of animals and birds. He often showed visitors his elephants, camels, wild asses, apes and dogs, as well as his falcons, pigeons and other birds.

Nana is also said to have been fond of European society. He often extended hospitality to the English officers posted at Kanpur and entertained them lavishly. One of his visitors always regarded him as 'one of the best and most hospitable natives in the Upper Provinces'. Martin in *The Indian Empire* says, 'he gave sumptuous entertainments, made hunting parties for strangers of distinction and was always ready to lend his elephants and his equipages also for the use of the neighbouring sahibs and mem sahibs'. Interestingly, Nana was a good billiards player. It is believed that sometimes he would allow his opponent to win the game out of sheer politeness.

Although a generous host, Nana tended to remain aloof and hardly spoke to his guests. A visitor wrote of a large party at Bithur in the winter of 1851-52 for some residents of Kanpur, which lasted a whole day and continued till late at night. Nana Saheb, though appeared only for about half an hour. The guests were entertained to breakfast, lunch, dinner, archery and a ball in the evening.

An oft-repeated quote of the writer John Lang states:

> I sat down to a table twenty feet long … which was covered with a damask table cloth of European manufacture, but instead of a dinner napkin there was a bedroom towel. The soup was served up in a trifle dish which had formed part of a dessert service belonging to the 9th Lancers – at all events the arms of that regiment were upon it, but the plate into which I ladled it was of the old willow pattern. The *pilao*, which followed the soup, was served upon a huge plated dish, but the plate from which I ate it was of the very commonest description. The spoon and fork were silver … the pudding was brought in upon a soup plate of blue and gold pattern … The cool claret I drank out of a richly cut champagne glass and the beer out of an American tumbler of the very worst quality.

Thus while Nana extended his hospitality to the English officers of Kanpur, these friends could not reciprocate his kindness in like manner, as he would not dine or drink with them. However, 'he won the good opinion of the local officials and when the crisis came they turned to him for help and support'.

After Baji Rao's death, Nana Saheb kept pressing the government for the continuance of his father's pension or a part of it. The number of Baji Rao's followers living on his *jagir* was estimated at 15,000 in 1847. Nana had to cut down on this staff drastically, but many were old and had no means to support themselves. In 1851, Nana Saheb again represented to the government for the reconsideration of the issue of the allowance. He cited instances of states such as Gwalior, Indore, Bharatpur, Nagpur, Banda, and Bhopal. The rulers of some of these states were part of the Maratha Empire and under the rule of the Peshwa. Thus, while they and their descendents continued to enjoy liberal monetary support from the government, Nana, son and heir of the late Peshwa, was denied this, which was manifestly a gross injustice. In a subsequent communication, Nana pointed out that even the adopted sons of sovereign princes, in states such as

Nagpur, Bhore, and Phalton, were regarded as rightful heirs by the East India Company.

However, none of these communications and appeals had any effect on the authorities. They pointed out that the Peshwa had received an annual stipend of £8,00,000 besides the proceeds of his *jagir*. During the thirty years, the Peshwa had received the enormous sum of more than £2,50,00,000. He should thus have made ample provision for his family.

It is, however, difficult to say whether Baji Rao had saved enough for his family. According to an official estimate, the property he left behind did not exceed ₹ 30 lakh. From this, Nana had to maintain the large establishment of his father and support his numerous dependents. During his lifetime, Baji Rao had been exempt from the jurisdiction of the ordinary law courts. In 1852, this regulation was repealed and this reduced Nana and his brother to the status of common men and exposed them to the prospect of being dragged to a court of law. Another issue that caused distress to the oversensitive Nana was that he was disallowed the use of his father's seal. All these were unwelcome reminders of his reduced status, which added to the bitterness of the loss of pension. The world for Nana had changed.

After his representations fell on deaf ears, Nana felt that Lord Dalhousie would not change his mind and therefore he decided to appeal to a higher authority, the Court of Directors in London. However, Nana's memorial of December 1852 to the court did not produce any effect. It declined to accede to this request, and the authorities informed him that the court had decided that he had 'no claim whatsoever' to the pension and that his application was 'wholly inadmissible'. However, Nana Saheb did not give up hope and in 1853 forwarded another memorial to the Court of Directors, which met the same fate as the directors saw no reason to change their previous decision.

Nana still did not regard the case as closed. There was a practice of sending agent to London to represent cases. The Rani of Jhansi had done so, as had the Emperor of Delhi. The person Nana selected to argue his case in London was Azimullah. He was the most interesting and remarkable character. He was a man of humble origins and little is known of his early life. Mowbray Thompson, a young officer of the Native Infantry, says:

> Azimoolah was originally a *Khitmutgahr* (waiter at table) in some Anglo-Indian family; profiting by the opportunity thus afforded to him, he acquired a thorough acquaintance with the English and French languages, so as to be able to read and converse fluently and write accurately in both. He afterwards became a pupil and subsequently a teacher, in the Cawnpore government school and from the last named position he moved to become the *munshi* of Brigadier Scott and finally he was selected as the *vakeel* (prime agent) of the Nana.

Azimullah was a handsome man, to which he added, by his own efforts, cultivated manners. He arrived in London in 1854 and gave the impression that he was an Indian prince. He was received in high society and 'made himself extremely conspicuous in the parks and Belgravian drawing rooms and extremely troublesome at the public offices' (the latter, I presume, while arguing Nana's case). He was very popular with the fair maidens as well as the elderly matrons of British aristocracy. Love letters written to him by more than one lady were discovered later at Nana's residence. Fred Roberts, in his *Letters Written during the Indian Mutiny,* states, 'Azimullah's love affairs in England caused the greatest resentment among English officers in India.' Lord Roberts wrote to his sister on 31 December 1857:

> while searching over the Nana's Palaces at Bithur the other day, we found heaps of letters directed to that fiend Azimullah Khan by ladies in England, some from Lady ---, ending Your affect. Mother. Others, from a young girl at Brighton named ---, written in the most lovable manner. Such rubbish I never read, partly in French, which this scoundrel seems to have understood; how English ladies can be so infatuated. Miss ---- was going to marry Azimullah and I have no doubt, would like to still, although he was the chief instigator in the Cawnpore massacres.

However, Azimullah's success in the boudoir in London could not be repeated in his main mission, which was to press the claims of his master. He was assisted by an Englishman named Biddle, but could not cut much ice with the Court of Directors. He went up to the Queen's advisers but his pleas did not find much favour with them either. After a stay of almost two years, he decided to return home. But on the way, he stopped over at Constantinople as he wanted to go to Crimea 'to see the great *Roostums*, the Russians who had beaten the French and British armies together.' In Constantinople, he met the famous correspondent of the *Times,* W.H. Russel, who described Azimullah as 'a handsome slim young man of dark olive complexion, dressed in an Oriental costume and covered with rings and finery'. Russel goes on to add, 'he saw the British army in a state of depression and he formed a very unfavourable opinion of its morale and physique in comparison with that of the French.'

Meanwhile, Nana was living at Bithur and leading the life of a well-to-do Indian prince. He was always referred to as 'Maharaja', not only by the Indians, but also by the Europeans at Kanpur. The government did not, however, agree to the use of this title as it evidently felt that this could create complications and Nana Saheb's attempts to secure his father's pension probably increased their fear.

Kanpur was an important town with a population of 60,000 and was situated on the bank of the Ganges, which during the rainy season, was one and a half kilometres broad. Unlike Delhi, Benaras, Lucknow and Agra, it had no fine buildings as it had no comparable past, being merely an East India Company garrison town. The river could be crossed by a bridge of boats over which passed a ceaseless throng of travellers, camels, bullock carts, and horses. Life for the Europeans in Kanpur was very similar to that in other stations in north India. It revolved around churches, theatre, and clubs. The officials lived in large white-washed colonial bungalows in spacious compounds. There was the usual routine of cricket, races, whist parties, and balls. The town offered a pleasant life for a young subaltern or an aged colonel in the tropics.

The British frontier had moved westwards and there had been the war with the Sikhs. However, Kanpur was still an important military station as it commanded the Grand Trunk Road, as well as the highways to Awadh. It was therefore strongly garrisoned. It had European artillerymen with six cannons and other British regiments, making a total of about 300 combatants. Against this, there were three Indian regiments and some cavalry and artillerymen. Their numbers were estimated at 3,000. Kanpur also had several hundred Europeans and Anglo Indians working in civilian jobs.

The man in command at Kanpur was Major General Sir Hugh Wheeler. He was then about seventy years old and had served for more than fifty years in the army, almost all this time in India. He had distinguished himself in Afghanistan and during the Sikh Wars and his reputation as a soldier was high. He had married an Indian lady and loved India. He spoke Hindustani very well and was very popular with the sipahis. Although a short, spare man, not imposing in appearance, he was physically fit and had never been on medical leave.

When news of the uprising at Meerut and Delhi reached Kanpur, there was not much anxiety in the town. It was believed that General Wheeler's long experience and popularity would stand him in good stead and he would be able to avert any uprising at Kanpur. People were more in fear of the *goonda*s and unruly elements who inhabited the town and gave it an unsavoury reputation. Thus, in the early stages there was no panic and Wheeler's correspondence with Calcutta suggested that all was well. This tone, however, changed in the next few days when Wheeler was constrained to report that there was 'a good deal of excitement and alarm'.

General Wheeler's responsibility was to protect not only the families of the British troops in Kanpur, but also the large colony of Europeans and Eurasians. Many of these had provided themselves with boats so that if there was trouble, they could escape by the river. Others had Indian dresses made for themselves and their women, and it was one of those times when having a dark skin was not a disadvantage.

On 22 May, about 55 Europeans and 240 *sowar*s (mounted soldiers) of the Oudh Irregular Cavalry arrived from Lucknow to assist Wheeler. Consequently, the sipahis of the Indian regiments became restive and rumours ran thick and fast that 'the *Saheb log* (officers) intended some mischief'. The men of the Indian Cavalry then enquired of the infantry whether they could count on their support should any attempt be made to dismount and disarm them.

Meanwhile, Wheeler met a deputation of civilian Europeans and Eurasians, and advised them to arm themselves, as well as assured them that in the event of an uprising, shelter would be provided at the military barracks. A welcome development for the English was that Nana Saheb had sent about 300 men, mostly Marathas, and two guns to serve them. But contrary to English calculations, the Marathas fraternized with the Hindu and Muslim sipahis and caused more uneasiness.

It is not clear whether Nana volunteered his services to the British or whether his help was sought by the civil authorities of Kanpur. In any case, it seems that the authorities had much confidence in him and Nana's offer of protecting the Treasury was accepted, whereupon Nana marched with 500 colourfully-dressed horsemen carrying lances and swords and long matchlocks, and took over the guardianship of the Treasury. This place contained a huge treasure estimated at more than £100,000.

Wheeler then organized the entrenchment at the barracks. These consisted of two main buildings, one with a thatched roof and the other with masonry, each able to accommodate 100 men. There were also some outhouses and half-finished barracks. Around the entrenchment, a trench was made that was not very deep and the earth thrown outside was used as a parapet.

The building of the entrenchment caused much resentment among the sipahis who felt it was tangible evidence that they were not trusted. The entrenchment was, however, not a strong position. It was suggested to Wheeler that it would be far better to take up a defensive position within the sturdy walls of the Magazine. But he declined to do so for fear lest, by removing the sipahis on guard already, he would provoke the collision he was so anxious to avoid. Besides, it was his firm belief that even if the sipahis did revolt, they would march straight to Delhi rather than trouble themselves with the Europeans at Kanpur. The withdrawal to the barracks would thus only be a temporary expedient and after the sipahis had left for Delhi, Wheeler thought that he could march to Allahabad with all his people. He was proved bitterly wrong on this count.

Captain Fletcher Hayes, who came with the Oudh troops to assist Wheeler at Kanpur had much to criticize. In a private letter to the Secretary of the Government of India, quoted by both Kaye and Malleson, he wrote:

> Since I have been in India I have never witnessed so frightful a scene of confusion, fright and bad arrangement as the European barracks presented. Four guns were in position loaded, with European Artillery men in night caps ... hanging to the guns in groups. People of all kinds, of every colour, sect and profession, were crowding into the barracks. Whilst I was there, buggies, *palki gharries*, vehicles of all sorts, drove up and discharged cargoes of writers, tradesmen and a miscellaneous mob of every complexion, from white to tawny – all in terror of the imaginary foe; ladies sitting down at the rough mess tables in the barracks, women suckling infants, ayahs and children in all directions and officers too ... I saw quite enough to convince me that if any insurrection took or takes place, we still have no one to thank but ourselves, because we have now shown to the natives how easily we can become frightened and when frightened utterly helpless.

Azimullah rather aptly labelled the entrenchment as 'the fort of despair'.

The spark for the mutiny was provided by a drunken officer who fired an ill-aimed shot at a patrol of the 2nd Cavalry who had challenged him as he staggered out of his bungalow in the dark. He was court-martialled but was let off on the grounds that his intoxication excused his conduct and that his firearm had gone off by mistake. This was a novel plea, for drunkenness is not a valid excuse in law and this palpable injustice confirmed the sipahis' suspicions that their officers meant some serious harm. The sipahis of the 2nd Cavalry 'muttered angrily that possibly their own muskets may go off by mistake before very long … if we natives had fired upon a European we would have been hanged.'

Meanwhile, open mutiny had broken out in Lucknow on 30 May. The next day, Wheeler received provisions of food, etc. at the entrenchment, as well as money from the Treasury. All this served as a signal for the mutiny. The Indian troop had also heard that reinforcements of European soldiers were expected in Kanpur and they decided to act before this happened.

The uprising finally took place on 5 June and, as expected, the 2nd Cavalry took the lead. They were soon joined by two infantry regiments, the 1st Infantry and the 56th Infantry. They seized the elephants from the cattle yard and marched to the Treasury under Teeka Singh and plundered it. Subedar Major Bhawani Singh tried to stop them but was overpowered and wounded. They then unlocked the doors of the jail and set fire to various other buildings. Then they took possession of the Magazine where many cannons and ammunition was stored. Wheeler had planned to blow up the Magazine but could not carry it through.

Meanwhile, the 53rd Infantry remained unaffected and was getting its breakfast ready when, inexplicably, General Wheeler ordered a battery to open fire on them. Mowbray Thompson writes, 'The 53rd remained, till by some error of the General, they were fired into. I am at an utter loss to account for this proceeding. The men were peacefully occupied in their lines, cooking; no signs of mutiny …' The 53rd were soon with the mutineers.

P.C. Gupta in his *Nana Sahib and the Rising at Kanpur* wrote: 'From the part subsequently played by Nana Saheb in the Mutiny, some of his earlier actions have acquired a sinister meaning.' William Howard Russell, a correspondent for the *Times*, wrote that 'Shortly before the Mutiny, Nana Saheb and Azimullah went to Lucknow and were reported to have exhibited considerable insolence and hauteur towards the Europeans they met there. Then they joined in a holy excursion, visited all the military stations all along the main trunk road, and went as far as Umballah.' Kaye has similarly stated, 'Early in 1857, after visiting Kalpi, Nana went to Delhi … For months, for years indeed, Nana and Azimullah had been quickly spreading their network of intrigue all over the country.' Other writers have made similar statements.

It is said that Nana wrote to all the native princes to support the revolt. After the unjust annexation of Awadh, he received replies to his communications from several of them. He also corresponded with Bahadur Shah Zafar, Gulab Singh of Jammu and the Government of Russia. The Russians are believed to have replied that no help could be given to him until he occupied Delhi and if he could succeed in that, assistance would be given to throw the English out.

P.C. Gupta, however, dismisses this interesting account as unreliable because 'there is hardly anything in official records or in documents captured at Bithur' to corroborate it and most of it is based on the testimony of one person, Sitaram. It is only about Nana's trip to Lucknow that we have firm evidence.

Having captured the Treasury and the Magazine, a deputation of mutineers called upon Nana Saheb, who seems to have soon made up his mind that he had no longer anything to gain by supporting the British. The sipahis needed a leader of high rank and the leader of the deputation said to him, 'Maharaj, a kingdom awaits you if you join our enterprise, but death, if you side with our enemies.' Nana immediately replied, 'The British are no concern of mine. I only pretended to help them, at heart I am their mortal enemy ... I am altogether yours.'

On the other hand, Tatya Tope, in his last deposition gave a different version and had stated that Nana had been forced to join the sipahis' cause and assume their command. At first he refused to go to Delhi or to fight the British troops in Kanpur but later yielded to force. There may also be some truth in this and it may be remembered that the Maratha troops Nana had initially sent to help the British had fraternized with the sipahis, which may also have forced his hand. After the mutiny had been put down and Nana had escaped to Nepal, he wrote to the government that he had 'joined the rebels from helplessness'.

Apart from plundering the Treasury and destroying public offices, the sipahis did not do much damage to the city. They were not really organized but felt that, like their comrades at Meerut, they should also march to Delhi. This is what Wheeler had anticipated and many of the Europeans felt that as the sipahis had started their march, the danger was over and some even left the entrenchment and returned to their homes.

According to some accounts, after Nana had agreed to join the sipahis, they asked him to lead them to Delhi, which was the main theatre of war. The next morning, the four regiments took the Delhi road but they had gone no further than Kalyanpur when they decided to return. It is said that Nana's advisors, principally Azimullah, told him that he must not go to Delhi as there he would, at best, play a minor part, but at Kanpur, he would be the principal player. This shrewd argument made sense as the four mutinous regiments were expected to rally around him in the city and make short work of the *firanghees*, after which Nana would be in complete control of the whole area. The march was thus halted at Kalyanpur and, unexpectedly, the mutineers came back to Kanpur. Nana also wrote to General Wheeler that he was going to attack the entrenchment. It is difficult to explain why Nana notified Wheeler, in writing, of his intention to assault the entrenchment.

Wheeler was far from ready to resist any attack. He had always been convinced that the mutineers would make for Delhi. Now that they had turned on him, there was little hope of surviving, unless help came quickly. Before the entrenchment was cut off, Wheeler sent a last anguished message to Lucknow. 'British spirit alone remains,' he wrote, 'but it cannot last for ever. Surely we are not to die like rats in a cage.'

The entrenchment, or as Azimullah had described it, 'the fort of despair' had about 1,000 people, including women and children. There were 200 British soldiers and another 100 British officers from the Indian regiments, while the rest included civilians and a few *sipahi*s and servants who had chosen to stay with their employers. They were well supplied with muskets and ammunition, there being up to ten loaded muskets available for every man, should an assault be made on the entrenchment. They also had about eight or ten cannons, most of them nine pounders, but all of them were in dangerously exposed positions and the British gunmen found themselves targets for the sipahi musketry. Sir Hugh Wheeler was too old to bear the full brunt of the fight and the main responsibility of conducting the defense fell on the younger, but nonetheless capable, shoulders of Captain John Moore.

The entrenchment was cannonaded by the Indian troops day after day, but though the advantage of numbers was definitely on the rebels' side, a general assault was never attempted, possibly because it was commonly believed that the area had been heavily mined. Nana did not exercise effective control over the sipahis and the attack on the entrenchment was not always carried on with enthusiasm. Colonel Williams observed that the troops 'did just as they pleased, manned the attacking batteries and joined in the assaults or not as they deemed fit, the greater portion taking their ease, lounging in the bazaars and on the banks of the canal and plundering the provisions as they were brought into the city'. But the fire from the rebels had its effect on the barracks. Mowbray Thompson said, 'After a day or two of sharp cannonading, to which we were exposed, all the doors, windows and framework of this, the best of the two structures, were entirely shot away.'

Nana decided to command the battery in person. He soon felt that the guns were too far to be accurate and he moved his eighteen pounders closer to the entrenchment. He stayed at Duncan's Hotel, which was near the guns and about a kilometre from the entrenchment.

At the hotel, Nana Saheb began to plan his future regime as the new Peshwa. First, he reorganized the army, putting Teeka Singh of the 2nd Cavalry in command. In every regiment, infantry or cavalry, the top officers were assigned specific duties and pay scales of all the ranks were fixed. A superficial resemblance to the army organization of the Marathas in Shivaji's time was noticeable. Among the rebel leaders was Ramachandra Panduranga, better known as Tatya Tope, who was later to distinguish himself as one of the most talented leaders.

A proclamation was made that the Peshwa's rule had begun. This was done by beating drums through the town. Next, the civil administration was reorganized. Criminal justice was to be dispensed by Nana's brother, Baba Bhat. Thieves and other malefactors were produced before him and duly punished. But the penalties imposed were not those sanctioned by the erstwhile law of British India. The

Hindu Criminal law, with which the Maratha judicial officers were familiar, was revived. So the culprits were sentenced to mutilation and their limbs were removed. All this is not to suggest that Nana was trying to revive a purely Hindu state. At the outbreak of the mutiny, not only the *Mahavir Jhanda* of the Hindus, but also the green banner of the Muslims was unfurled. There was no conflict between the faiths. They all wanted the common enemy out and the restoration of old institutions.

Nana's establishment of the courts of justice and appointment of a *Kotwal* was an attempt to bring about some law and order in Kanpur. The city ruffians, of which there was no dearth, were busy plundering and setting fire to property owned by Europeans. The shops were also being looted and there was confusion all over. Some semblance of order was restored so that regular supplies of food could be maintained for Indian troops, as well chemicals for the production of gunpowder.

From documents later discovered in Gwalior, it appears that Nana Saheb's ambitions were not limited to the establishment of his rule at Kanpur. He envisaged holding sway over huge tracts of India, which would be divided into *suba*s (provinces) for each of which the revenue was estimated. Another absurd document mentions the amount of tribute that would be levied on kings, princes and rajas of India, as well as tribute from several foreign countries.

While the outline of the new administration was being made, Nana was also trying to strengthen his grip on the entrenchment, but he did not have effective control over the sipahis and they did as they pleased. However, finally, their firing and cannonading had its effect. A shell fired from the battery set afire the thatched roof of one of the barracks. The roof was as dry as tinder and the breeze spread the conflagration, causing considerable damage. The sipahi who had fired the shot received a 'reward of ₹ 90 and a shawl'.

Life in the entrenchment was a story of terrible human suffering and endurance. While there was no dearth of arms and ammunition, there was a tremendous shortage of food and water. Lieutenant Mowbary Thompson wrote of comical scenes in the first few days, when one could see a private carrying 'a bottle of champagne, a tin of preserved herrings and a pot of jam while another was walking along with salmon, rum and sweet meats'. But this did not last more than a week and everyone 'was reduced to the monotonous and scanty allowance of one meal a day consisting of a handful of split peas and a handful of flour'. Sometimes, when the cavalry came within range, a horse was shot and provided a meal. On another occasion, a bull came grazing within gun shot and was eagerly brought down. A dog, a highly prized delicacy, was successfully targeted. It was easier to kill these animals than to transport the carcasses within the walls and sometimes the foreigners attempting this were also shot down by the sipahis.

There was only one well with water in the entrenchment and as it was in an exposed position, it was extremely dangerous to draw water there by day. There was a second well, but it was dry, and used as a cemetery. The stench in the entrenchment was fearful and several women, unable to bear it, got into craters in the compound, where many died of the heat, as it was the height of summer. The death toll was high, not only from the cannonade and gunfire, but also from illness. The fifty-nine trained artillery men had all been killed during the first week and had to be replaced by infantry officers and even civilians.

General Wheeler, looking 'very feeble and aged', issued orders lying on a mattress. His Indian wife and daughter sat in another corner of the room. Wheeler had tried to send several messages to Lucknow for help but the Indian messengers could not get through. Finally, an Englishman disguised as an Indian was sent 'but having been given too much rum to fortify him at the time of departure, he was rather drunk when he left and soon fell into the hands of the enemy'. A message did eventually reach Lucknow, but General Sir Henry Lawrence could do nothing to help, as the rebels commanded the river and a crossing was not possible. So the defenders abandoned any hope of aid.

From time to time, spies brought in news of the entrenchment to Nana Saheb. On a couple of occasions, the enemy had captured some sipahis, but all of them managed to escape. Wheeler felt that this was dangerous as they would carry tales of the misery and helplessness in the entrenchment. So it was decided that if any prisoners were taken, they would be killed outright. Nana, on another occasion, sent a man dressed as a water carrier who appeared to be a friend of the British. He brought the false news that troops to help them were across the river. He came a second time the next day and eventually the British realized that he was one of Nana's spies sent to find out the state of things in the entrenchment and feed the defenders false information.

Nana Saheb was unhappy with the state of affairs. He had been told that the surrender of the British was a matter of a few days. They had, however defended themselves for weeks and, though they had been badly battered, he did not know how long they would be able to resist. It may be remembered that Nana did not have complete control over the rebels and sometimes his orders were just ignored. A few half-hearted attempts had been made to assault the entrenchment but without success. In one, eighteen men had been killed and the rest retreated. Another attack by the cavalry and infantry was also beaten back by the firing from the entrenchment cannons. In yet another advance, the sipahis approached the entrenchment pushing in front of them large bales of cotton to serve as cover. This measure deadened the effects of the shots to some extent and they managed to approach close. But the cannon balls soon set fire to the bales of cotton and the attack was never pressed home.

The failure of these attacks due to the British cannons was a disappointment for Nana Saheb. The numbers were all in favour of the rebels but they had not launched a general assault. After these failed attempts, it was felt that the only option was to starve the enemy into surrender. Kanpur was closed to the rest of British India and supplies could not be obtained. The bridge of boats had been destroyed, telegraph lines were cut and all fords on the river were guarded.

Nana was joined by a wealthy Muslim of Kanpur, Mohammad Ali Khan – better known as Nane Nawab – who was placed in charge of the battery near the Racquets Court. He established his headquarters at the courts and soon this became the favourite haunt of the troops, as the best-known courtesan of Kanpur, Azizun, used to entertain them here every evening. Nana Saheb had by now moved from Duncan's Hotel and lived in a large tent on the grounds facing the entrenchment. Here he used to hold consultations with Teeka Singh and the Muslim leaders. The troops were, however, not pursuing the siege with much vigour and by the third week of June, the leaders decided to bring the operations to a close.

On 25 June, the British saw a woman approaching the entrenchment. A soldier was about to shoot her down when Mowbray Thomson knocked down his arm and let her come. He recognized her as Mrs Greenway, the Eurasian wife of a wealthy local merchant. Others identified her as Mrs Jacobi, also a Eurasian woman. Whoever she was, she handed over to Mowbray Thomson a letter addressed to the 'Subjects of the Most Gracious Majesty Queen Victoria'. It read; 'All those who are in no way connected with the acts of Lord Dalhousie, and are willing to lay down their arms, shall receive a safe passage to Allahabad.' The letter was not signed but the handwriting was recognized as that of Azimullah.

General Wheeler was still expecting relief from Calcutta and was reluctant to agree. He was also suspicious of Nana's intentions. Captain Moore prudently pointed out that once the rainy season, already overdue, began, it would be impossible to hold out. The rains would wash away the well, flood the trenches and dampen the gunpowder. The women and children were suffering dreadfully and, in any case, there was hardly any food left. Wheeler was finally persuaded to agree to surrender.

Soon Azimullah and Jawala Prasad came to the entrenchment to discuss terms. It was agreed that the entrenchment would be evacuated; each man would be permitted to leave with his arms and sixty rounds of ammunition. Conveyance would be provided for the wounded, the women and children and boats would be kept ready at the *ghat*s with a sufficient supply of food. The treaty of capitulation was signed by Nana, and Jawala Prasad came to the British camp with two other persons as hostages for Nana's good faith. The British cannons were surrendered and three officers, including Lieutenant Delafosse, were escorted to the riverside to see that the boats were in readiness.

On the morning of 27 June, sixteen elephants and seventy to eighty palanquins came to carry the fugitives to the boats. The women and children were carried by elephants or in bullock carts, while the able-bodied walked. Everyone could not be accommodated and the evacuation could only be completed after Captain Moore made a second trip. General Wheeler, who was old and ill, and his wife and daughter had to walk down to the boats. The fugitives were in a sorry state; the children were weak and emaciated, the women in rags and the soldiers in tattered uniforms. There was a huge crowd of Kanpur citizens, who lined the way to the *ghat*s and waited at the riverside to see their erstwhile rulers depart. While the spectators were merely curious, there were several sipahis and others who had come to see their officers or their employers for the last time. No foreigner was molested and it was interesting to note that many sipahis treated their officers with consideration, carrying and loading their baggage in bullock carts. They helped Major Vibart and his family down to the boats 'with the most profuse demonstration of respect'. Similarly, many servants, who could not see their old masters, appealed to the rebel soldiers to pay their respects.

It was late summer and the water in the river was low. It was necessary to climb down the high bank and wade through the water to reach the boats. All the foreigners had embarked and were waiting to move off. What happened next was believed at the time to be 'so foul an act of treachery the world had never seen'. But as Michael Edwards says in *Red Year*, 'it is more likely that it was one of those ghastly accidents that splatter the pages of history and on which any interpretation suitable to the needs of the occasion can be imposed. Probably a musket shot was heard and the British, fearful of treachery and with nerves frayed by three weeks of constant siege, immediately opened fire.'

Mowbray Thomson, who was in the midst of it all, describes the events in this manner:

> At a signal from the shore, the native boatmen who numbered eight, all jumped over and waded to the shore. We fired into them immediately but the majority of them escaped. Before they quitted

> us, these men had contrived to secrete burning charcoal in the thatch of most of our boats. Simultaneously with the departure of the boatmen, the identical troopers who had escorted Major Vibart to the *ghat* opened fire on us with carbines. As well as the confusion, caused by the burning of the boats would allow, we returned the fire of the horsemen, who were about fifteen in number, but they retired immediately after the volley they had given us.
>
> ...
>
> Those of us who were not disabled by wounds now jumped out of boats and endeavoured to push them afloat; but alas! Most of these were utterly immovable. Now from the ambush, in which they were all concealed all along the bank, it seems that thousands of men fired upon us; besides four nine pounders, carefully masked and pointed to the boats, every bush was filled with sepoys.

At the Satichaura Ghat there was absolute pandemonium. There was a large crowd of civilians on the river bank and as soon as the firing started, they scattered fast or were pushed back by the cavalry. Many of the British in the boats were shot dead as they jumped into the water to escape the flames. Out of the forty boats at the *ghat* only three succeeded in getting away, two of these soon floundered and one boat on which Delafosse and Mowbray Thomson found a place, were overcrowded with the wounded.

From the accounts available it is not clear who fired the first shot. Was it the man from Mowbray Thomson's boat or the horsemen on the banks? Thomson clearly states that when the boatmen jumped overboard they were fired upon and some were killed. So the first shots may have been fired by the British. At the same time, it must be accepted that guns and troops had been posted on the river banks.

Another question is what was Nana's role in this massacre? It is difficult to answer. He was the head of the rebel army and so cannot be absolved from all responsibility. But John Lang could not believe that Nana was responsible for the incident at Satichaura Ghat. He states:

> In the absence of some proof I should be sorry – especially after the letters I have read on the subject to attribute to the man that fiendish

> treachery and horrible massacre which took place at Cawnpore in July 1857. Nana Saheb had seen so much of English gentlemen and ladies and was personally, if not intimately, acquainted with so many of the sufferers, that it is only fair to suppose, when he ordered boats to be ready, he was sincere in his desire that the Christians should find their way to Calcutta and that what ensured was in violation of his orders, and the acts of those who wished to place for ever between Nana Saheb and the British government an impassable barrier, so far as peace and reconciliation were concerned. No one knew better than Nana Saheb that in the event of the British becoming again the conquerors of India, the very fact of his having spared the lives of those who surrendered, would have led to the sparing of his own life and hence the promise that he made to Sir Hugh Wheeler.

Colonel Maude, writing a few years later, doubted whether Nana Saheb was 'guilty of complicity in the murders of our women and children'. Maude was rather of the opinion that 'his hand though guilty, was forced by his more bloodthirsty followers, whose acts he dared not disavow'.

Dr S.N. Sen says, 'If Nana mediated treachery from the first, one wonders why so much money and labour were wasted on the boats, as once out of the entrenchment, the English would be as helpless in the midst of a hostile crowd on land, as they were on the river.'

It must be understood that stories of Colonel James Neill's diabolical atrocities had already reached the sipahis and the citizens of Kanpur. Colonel Neill was a Scotsman aged forty-seven with thirty years of military service behind him. He arrived in Benaras in May 1857 with the 1st Madras Fusiliers and unleashed the most hideous terror in the area. Village after village was burnt down. As the inhabitants tried to run out, Neill placed a ring of troops around, with orders to shoot down every man, woman and child. In addition, 'Neill's hangings' were notorious and wherever he was, it was a common sight to see corpses hanging from trees and signposts. He was a religious man and all this madness, in his perverted view, was 'holy work'. It is likely that the massacre at Satichaura was inspired by reports of Neill's diabolical actions.

Reverting to the scene at Satichaura Ghat, as mentioned earlier one of the boats got away. It was followed by the rebels riding alongside on the river banks and many more fugitives were killed. Finally, after two days, some of them left the boat, swam ashore and made for Allahabad on foot, fighting off rebels and avoiding the river crocodiles. Many of their number were lost, until there were only four left: Mowbray Thomson, Delafosse and two others. Thomson was left with only a shirt, Delafosse had a cloth around his waist while the other two were naked. They were eventually saved by the protection of a local zamindar of Awadh, Digvijaya Singh, who kept them at his residence.

After the massacre at the Satichaura Ghat, there were several survivors still in the water. They were all brought to the river bank and the men were all separated and shot. There were approximately 125 surviving women and children. Their jewellery was snatched, their dresses torn and many were wounded. But Nana's men then took charge and orders were given that they should be molested no more. They were taken to Savada House and later moved to another house, originally built by a British officer for his Indian mistress, and known as Bibighar. Here they were joined by a few officers and several women and children who had fled from Fatehgarh and other towns, thinking that they could find refuge at Kanpur.

At the end of June, Nana Saheb held a military parade to celebrate the successful termination of the siege of the entrenchment. From some of the detachments who had mutinied, several soldiers had dispersed into the countryside as they felt it was the end of the action and the British had been expelled. But there were still six complete infantry and two cavalry regiments on the parade ground. Nana appeared to a twenty-one gun salute and distributed large sums of money to the sipahis. Two days later, Nana proceeded to Bithur, where he was installed on his father's throne as Peshwa and the consecration mark was fixed on his forehead. Proclamations were made to the people that 'all Christians who had been at Delhi and other places had been destroyed … And that the yellow faced and narrow-minded people had been conquered at Kanpur, it was the duty of all subjects of the new government to rejoice and to carry on their work and to be obedient to the present government.' But contrary to expectations, Nana's rule was to last for only a short time.

Although Wheeler had surrendered, the British at Calcutta were unaware of this and were still trying to make arrangements to reinforce him with European troops and guns. Neill was ordered to Kanpur, but was later superseded in command by General Henry Havelock, who arrived from Calcutta in Benaras on 28 June. He started his march towards Kanpur with a large body of European and Sikh soldiers. Renaud, another general, was already ahead of Havelock. A devilish man, he intended 'hanging all black creations', and traces of his passage through the area were evident: burnt villages and dead bodies swinging from trees, their lower portions eaten up by animals. Havelock overtook Renaud and the two joined forces, making the combined army a formidable one.

As they advanced to Kanpur, Nana's cavalry opposed them but found that they were at a disadvantage as the British fire from their Enfield rifles and cannons reached the cavalry at unexpected distances and blunted their charge. This forced them to withdraw, leaving twelve guns behind. Then followed a second battle on 15 July and on the same day the Pandu river was crossed by the enemy. It is difficult to explain why Nana had not destroyed the bridge. The passage was hotly fought over by his men but ultimately the enemy troops were within 30 kilometres of Kanpur. Nana was not prepared to abandon his headquarters without a fight and defended the entrance to the city with 5,000 men whom he led in person. This was a fierce battle and Nana's men fought every inch of the ground, but, unfortunately, his stand before Kanpur was as unsuccessful as the previous two.

After the massacre at Satichaura Ghat, the survivors along with the new refugees from Fatehpur and other towns, in all about 170, had all been lodged at Bibighar. The news that the battle of Pandu river had been lost and that Havelock would soon reach Kanpur led to the death of them all. The women and children had been kept alive so far with some idea of using them as hostages. But as the British moved towards Kanpur, they instituted such a reign of terror in the conquered areas, killing and murdering innocent people that as one writer put it 'they left the Indians no inducement to show mercy'. It was also feared that the prisoners would serve as witnesses and implicate many of the leading citizens. Reports also said that the British were coming like 'mad dogs' and some troopers suggested that 'If it was not for the women and children in confinement, the enemy soldiers would not rush on with such impetuosity. Why not kill the prisoners and let the British know of it, then you will find they will be discouraged and go back.' Thus, it could have been the result of such advice, or fear or rage at British bestiality, that it was decided to put all the survivors at Bibighar to death.

The four or five men there were taken out and shot, but the killing of the women and children presented a difficulty, for the sipahis were reluctant to obey orders and instead of aiming at them, 'they fired at the ceiling of the room'. A woman called Hussaini Khanum, popularly known as the 'Begum', who generally looked after the prisoners was asked to call some butchers from the bazaars. They had little compunction and drawing their swords and cleavers they cut down the prisoners. The next morning, the mangled remains of the bodies were thrown down the well in the compound.

There has been no evidence yet to link Nana directly to the massacre, but it seems improbable that he could have been ignorant of the decision taken. In this connection, I will quote the historian, Dr S.N. Sen:

> But on such evidence as was tendered before Colonel Williams, no criminal court would convict the most notorious malefactor. Absence of such reliable evidence however does not necessarily connote absence of guilt. Nana was legally and morally responsible for the lives of his prisoners and the massacre was committed in his name. Until it is conclusively proved that he had no knowledge of it, he cannot be absolved of the charge of connivance and must share the obloquy and opprobrium of that shameful act. Nana himself denied that he had ever committed any murder. In an *Ishtaharnama* addressed to Her Majesty the Queen, the Parliament, the Court of Directors, the Governor General and all offices and delivered to Major Richardson in April 1859 he asserted that he had nothing to

> do with killing of women and children. "At Cawnpore the soldiers and ryots disobeyed my orders and began killing the English women and children. All I could, I saved by any means."

As Havelock's army camped near Kanpur, Nana pulled back his troops into the city and then retreated further to Bithur. Nana now had little hope of putting up another fight and so he blew up the Magazine at Kanpur. Billowing smoke engulfed the city and rose high into the sky. There was a general exodus of the local population as the panic-stricken people tried to escape from the advancing enemy. They moved westward and took shelter in the countryside and the neighbouring villages. As expected, the enemy troops entering Kanpur took dreadful revenge; they killed and plundered indiscriminately. It took quite some time before law and order could be restored and Havelock had to issue orders that all British soldiers would be hung up on the gallows in their uniforms if they did not stop plundering and killing.

The British were apprehensive that Nana would attack Kanpur again but this proved to be baseless. Whatever troops Nana had left were soon dispersing into the country or returning to their villages. Nana then decided to cross the river and disappear into Awadh. In the third week of July, he and his family left Bithur in boats. To delude the enemy so that he would not be pursued, he spread the word that he was going to commit suicide by drowning in the river. As the boat approached midstream, its lights were extinguished; this was to suggest that he had thrown himself into the river. This story was even believed for a while and was confirmed by some clerks employed by the British, one of whom said, 'He had seen the end of Nana Saheb. When the British troops moved into Bithur he took his whole family out in the Ganges in a boat, knocked out a plank and went down with them all.' But in actual fact, he and his family crossed the river and disappeared from the scene in the dark of the night. Meanwhile, 'the mendicant Brahmins rushed into his palace and plundered all they could lay their hands on.'

Bithur was soon occupied by the enemy and a British soldier said, 'We looted a good deal and set fire to his palace.' Obviously, they did not do a good job and a month later British troops had to pull it down brick by brick. The animals in the menagerie were eagerly seized and the more exotic ones were taken to Calcutta and sold for lucrative amounts.

Havelock, meanwhile, also crossed into Awadh with his troops and Neill was left in charge at Kanpur. He immediately set about taking revenge for the massacre at Bibighar. He wrote in a letter which is quoted by Kaye, 'I will show to the natives of India that the punishment inflicted by us for such deeds will be the heaviest and the most revolting to their feelings and what they must ever remember.' Neill ordered all miscreants who took part in the mutiny be sentenced to death. But before they were strung up on the gallows, each man was made to clean up a small portion of the blood stains at Bibighar, and to make it as revolting to their feelings as possible, they were made to lick part of the blood with their tongues. To add to it all, Neill ordered that after they had been hung, all Hindus would be buried and all Muslims would be burned.

Nana Saheb, meanwhile, was in Awadh with his troops. His movements for the next few weeks are difficult to trace, but he did obstruct Havelock's columns advancing towards Lucknow and kept threatening his rear. He fought a few skirmishes and his troops resorted to some plundering. In late September, Havelock, reinforced by Neill's and Outram's troops, crossed the Ganges and, fighting his way through the streets of Lucknow, relieved the British at the Residency there. There was heavy loss of life on both sides. Neill was killed by a neatly placed shot through his head.

At this stage, Nana considered the possibility of escaping to Chandernagar, a French enclave in Bengal, but he could not get through the cordon of enemy troops. He then sent two of his agents to Chandernagar with a letter to Emperor Napoleon III asking for help against the British and 'dwelling on the iniquities of the foreign Government'. This letter was received in Paris, but no reply was sent.

In the winter of 1857-58, Kanpur was again threatened by the arrival of the Gwalior contingent, which had joined the rebels at Kalpi, not far from Kanpur. Campbell had marched to Lucknow, leaving General Charles Windham in command at Kanpur. Tatya Tope, at the head of the Gwalior contingent supported by Kunwar Singh's regiments, attacked the city and inflicted a crushing defeat on Windham. The British troops were panic stricken and fell back into the city and the entrenchment there. Tatya Tope held the town at his mercy.

On hearing this, the commander-in-chief, Sir Colin Campbell, hurriedly left Lucknow with a strong force and returned to Kanpur. In the ensuing battle, Tatya Tope could not hold the city and his troops were pushed back.

Soon after this, Brigadier Grant was sent to Bithur with a detachment and he completed the work of destruction that had earlier been half done by the British army. Nana's palace and his temple were burnt down. Some of his treasure was concealed in a well, deep in the water. The British drained out the water, and James Aberigh Mackay writing in *From London to Lucknow* says,

> Quantities of Nana's gold and silver plates have been got up out the well at Bithur since Christmas. The massive golden bowl weighs forty pounds. It is believed that twelve lakhs of rupees are buried in the same well ... The last day the Highland Brigade was encamped at Bithur, they got so much gold and silver in one of Nana's wells that one man could scarcely carry the load. They had previously obtained from the same well 75 pounds of gold and 252 pounds of silver.

At this stage, the British offered a reward for the capture of Nana. The National Achives of India, has this order:

> To Captain Bruce
> Illegible.....
> 15 Feb. 1858
>
> Sir,
> I am directed ...
> In reply I am ordered to state that you should assure all Zamindars and Talookdars who may have rendered us any active assistance

during the course of the rebellion that they are regarded with special favour by the Government and when the disturbances are quelled they will be put into a position at least as good as that they enjoyed prior to the annexation of Oudh.

A lac of rupees may be offered for the Nana, and pardon to any rebel not himself a participator in the atrocities who may give such information as could lead to his capture.

You are authorised to offer whatever reward you deem suitable for the apprehension of (name illegible) and other notorious rebels.

I have (rest illegible)
G. Couper
Secretary to the Chief Commissioner of Oudh

(Dept. Foreign – Cons. 26 March 1858 Nos 74, 78, SC).

The whereabouts of Nana Saheb between January and March 1858 are unknown. There are several intelligence reports of his movements in the National Archives, but these were subsequently contradicted. Reliable information was finally received that he was hiding in the small fort of Fathepur Chaurasi on the Ganges. Brigadier Grant followed him, but when he got there two days later, Nana had disappeared. He was chased by Grant's column towards Rohilkhand and at the end of September he was located at Shahjahanpur. By the time the enemy troops got there, he had again escaped. But before he departed, Nana's troops had destroyed every house in the cantonment, so that the pursuing army would not get any shelter there. For the next six months, Nana was a fugitive, keeping out of the reach of British troops. The commander-in-chief learnt late in December 1858 that Nana and thousands of sipahis and desperadoes had collected near Bankee. British troops marched through the night to catch Nana there. After brief firing from both sides, the rebel troops were pushed back in disorder towards the river Rapti. With no hope of success, Nana loaded eight elephants with treasure and swiftly retreated across the river. From there, both he and his brother, along with their families, escaped to Nepal. There are two more letters in the National Archives offering further rewards for the capture of Nana.

After this, the British army kept a close watch on the border passes to prevent Nana and his troops from crossing the border back into India. By the end of 1859, reports reached the Government of India that both Nana and his brother were dead.

In his move to Nepal, Nana Saheb had been accompanied by his wife Kasibai, his sister Sarasvatibai, his brother Bala Rao and his family and various other relatives. Azimullah also came with Nana along with thousands of sipahis. Begum Hazrat Mahal of Oudh was also believed to have entered Nepal with him.

Nana may have had to flee the country, but he left a huge impression behind. P.C. Gupta says:

> ... the story of Nana's life never ceased to excite popular imagination. In Europe also he had a large public. In English literature, Maude says, he was one of the "extraordinary monsters of ferocity and slaughter, but in the hands of the French, he became a scented sybarite, who read Balzac, played Chopin on the piano, and lolling on a divan, fanned by exquisite odalisques from Cashmere, had a roasted English child brought in occasionally on a pike for him to examine with his pince-nez." Jules Verne, in one of his lesser known novels, imagined Nana Saheb as a wandering fakir who returned to India a few years later and met an old enemy, a British officer near Aurangabad. It is difficult to say if Nana Saheb ever returned to India, but the last phase of his life was perhaps even more exciting than the French novelist had imagined.

In Nepal, Nana Saheb was met by a military officer on behalf of the government. He was told by Jung Bahadur, who ruled the country at the time, that Kasibai and the other lady members of the family would be given shelter and protection, but this would not include Nana Saheb himself. He was advised to quietly disappear, after which the Nepal authorities would not hunt him down.

Nana Saheb was disappointed at this cold reception, but he temporarily accepted the situation. He still had hopes of coming to some terms with the British government. He sent a letter to Major Richardson in Lucknow for onward transmission. It was addressed to

Queen Victoria and the British Parliament and the point Nana made in it was that he had been forced by the mutinous sipahis of the British army to join the revolt and if he had not, his family would have been killed by them. He went on to say that after the surrender by General Wheeler at Kanpur he had provided boats for their safe travel to Allahabad, but it was the sipahis of the British army that attacked them, while his troops had saved the lives of the survivors and given them shelter. He said that after he left Kanpur with his men, it was the rebel sipahis who killed them at Bibighar. He concluded the letter saying he was not a murderer. If the government would not appreciate his stand he would have no option but to continue the fight. He was just across the border and not any great distance from British forces, that his troops were not fully under his control and he had no country, but he would still prove a worthy enemy to so powerful a nation as Britain. Death would come to him, but he had no fear of that.

Major Richardson wrote back suggesting that if he had not committed murder, he should surrender without fear. But Nana could not consider surrender in this manner. He wanted an assurance from Her Majesty the Queen, after which he would surrender without hesitation. Some more correspondence followed and Nana was sent a copy of the Queen's Proclamation that laid down general terms for all offenders. This was unacceptable to Nana and the correspondence finally came to naught.

Nana, under the circumstances, decided that it was best to accept Jung Bahadur's terms and disappear from the scene. He then changed into the clothes of a mendicant and moved into western Nepal. During all his recent torturous travels in India, fighting skirmishes and evading the British hunt for him, he had still managed to bring with him to Nepal some valuable family heirlooms. Jung Bahadur, well informed about this, decided to take full advantage of Nana's helplessness by proposing to buy his jewels at a fraction of their real price. P.C. Gupta says,

> The most valuable ornament in Nana Saheb's possession was the *naulakha*, the principal jewel of the Peshwas, a long, necklace of pearls, diamonds and emeralds and for this Jung Bahadur offered a

> paltry 93,000 rupees. Later on a settlement was reached by which, in exchange for the necklace, he bestowed two villages to Kasibai. After paying the revenues she had an income of 6,000 to 7,000 rupees a year.

Despite Jung Bahadur's arm twisting, he got only a small part of the treasure Nana Saheb had brought with him from India. No one had any idea where he had hidden the rest of it. For several years after his entry into Nepal, he was able to maintain a large body of troops, arms and other equipment, as well as his retinue. This could only have been possible with the help of the treasure he had brought across the border. In 1957, exactly 100 years after the Revolt, the Nepal government launched a treasure hunt in the thickly wooded Nagarjun hill area, which is some distance away from Kathmandu. A large hoard of wealth in the shape of gold, silver and jewellery was rumoured to have been hidden in this area by Nana's widow and his followers. The government, however, has remained quiet on whether any treasure was found.

Kasibai was a young girl and lived in Kathmandu. Jung Bahadur had given her a house in the suburbs and also arranged an allowance of 400 rupees per month for her. As Nana's wife, she aroused much interest in the aristocracy of Nepal and had an eventful life. Jung Bahadur was a constant admirer, but apart from him, she seems to have had many other lovers. However, despite the fact that she was unfaithful to Nana, she retained much affection for him. Occasionally during some important festivals such as *Shivratri,* he managed to visit her secretly.

Following Jung Bahadur's instructions to disappear, Nana and his followers moved to the *terrai* (foothills). This was not a healthy place to live in, especially during the rainy season. By the end of 1859, it was reported that Bala Saheb, Nana's brother, and Azimullah had both died of fever and Nana was suffering from malaria. Many of his men were also stricken. Sometime later it was rumoured that Nana had also died. The British were still very interested in Nana's whereabouts and on getting these reports they considered the possibility that they were all false reports that had been deliberately planted to mislead then. They felt that Maharaja Jung Bahadur would know the truth, but he refused to comment. Meanwhile, further rumours about Nana's death kept pouring in, but the investigation of the British authorities led nowhere.

In 1860, a British planter was kidnapped by Nana's men. He was released several months later and on his return he said that he had been a prisoner in Nana Saheb's camp and had met both Nana and his brother. He went on to say that he had been forced to travel with Nana's party, which consisted of several hundred armed men for twenty days. After crossing Nepal's northern border, they had travelled in some part of Tibet. Some sipahis captured by the British near the Nepal border also confirmed that both, Nana and his brother were alive and in good health. They were dressed like fakirs and were accompanied by several hundred armed troops.

The British military, after sifting through all the evidence, came to the conclusion that the story of Nana's death 'was given out to favour his escape and aid his concealment'.

Nana was believed to be living on the Nepal border close to Kumaon, in present day Uttarakhand. He was later believed to have travelled to India with an entourage of more than 1,000 men. Between 1862 and 1874, several persons were arrested in India for their likeness to Nana Saheb. One man was arrested in Karachi and brought to Calcutta. In 1863, another man was caught in Ajmer as he resembled Nana and was about the same age, which was forty-five years. After much investigation, the authorities failed to identify him and he was released. Another 'Nana' was reported to have turned up in Mewar, but this also proved false.

In October 1874, a letter was brought to Maharaja Scindia of Gwalior, which was said to have been written by Nana Saheb. In it, he said, he had arrived in Gwalior after a long time spent in dangerous and distressing circumstances. He further said that since Scindia's ancestors had always been obedient to and well-wishers of Nana's own ancestors, the Peshwas, he had come for help and protection as he was now friendless and helpless. Maharaja Scindia immediately went with the bearer of the note to where Nana was staying. There he met a frail-looking man dressed as a monk. After questioning the man closely, Scindia brought him to the palace, where on further interrogation, Scindia was convinced that he had met the Peshwa. Scindia being a Scindia, promptly handed him over to the British political agent at Gwalior. Here, the man confessed to all Nana's crimes and explained his movements over the last sixteen years.

The arrest of Nana Saheb raised fears that this could rekindle the flame of rebellion and stir sympathy with the prisoner. He was therefore immediately shifted to Kanpur. But his identification proved as difficult as that of the previous suspects. British officials who had seen Nana at Kanpur in pre-mutiny days had immediate doubts that this prisoner was Nana. Mowbray Thomson, who had been in the entrenchment at Kanpur and was one of the few to escape on the boat, said this man was completely different from the man he remembered. This was a humble, cringing man and utterly different from the distant and impressive man he had originally seen. Almost thirty other witnesses came forward, including some relatives of Nana, but none were absolutely certain about the man. Meanwhile, the prisoner also retracted the confession he had made at Gwalior. It was also noted that even his handwriting bore no resemblance to the handwriting of Nana. Finally, General Sir Henry Daly concluded that the attempts to identify the man had failed.

A couple of theories were put forward. The first was that the real Nana was in Gwalior at the time and had sent one of his followers to actually test out Scindia's reaction: would he extend protection or would he be a traitor? The second was that Scindia had found the real Nana, but since the British government was not willing to spare the man's life, he had substituted an imposter before any foreigner in authority had seen him.

General Sir Henry Daly believed that the real Nana was alive and this belief was shared by many. In 1894, another man was arrested, but since then thirty-seven years had passed, no one had the faintest idea what Nana looked like. The ghost was thus finally laid to rest.

No one knows what happened to Nana Saheb. There are many loose ends in his story to which answers are still not available. Did he follow Jung Bahadur's advice to disappear in Nepal and die there of old age or did he return to India?

Nana Saheb was the man who organized the revolt in the United Provinces. He was the rallying point, not only for the sipahis, but also the landed aristocracy and their relatives and peasants. He gave them direction and channeled their efforts to curb British power. Although he was unsuccessful, he was the key figure in what has often been called the First War of Independence. He set an example and proved an inspiration to future generations who continued the struggle.

TATYA TOPE

A good biography of Tatya Tope, one of the most important leaders of the rebellion, is strangely, still missing. There are some short accounts in Hindi and Marathi but the ones in English are more a history of the rebellion, rather than the story of his life. All seem to be highly eulogistic but short on facts. One reason for this is the sheer lack of information about this elusive character. He was a modest man and his loyalty to Nana Saheb kept him from seeking the limelight. In contemporary official writing of the time, even the identity of Tatya Tope was a subject of wild speculation. In one government letter, he was stated to be a minister of the Baroda state, while in another communication, he was held to be identical with Nana Saheb. The National Archives has Tatya Tope's own statement, which he made on 10 April 1859, after his capture by the British. It gives an account of his activities during the last year or so of his life. But all he has to say about his family or his early life is contained in the first short paragraph of the statement and runs as follows: 'My name is Tatya Tope, my father's name is Pandurang, inhabitant of Jola Pargannah, Patoda Zillah, Nagar (Maharashtra). I am a resident of Bithur. I am about forty-five years of age, in the service of Nana Saheb in the grade of companion or "aide-de-camp".' Tatya's family was closely associated with Nana's father, Peshwa Baji Rao II. He and Nana grew up together at Bithur, had their education together and were good childhood friends.

Tatya Tope's full name was Ramchandra Pandurang Tope. Tatya Tope was a title; Tope means a commanding officer and is probably derived from the Hindi word *'tope'* which means a cannon or artillery. He was born in about 1814 and was executed on the gallows, when he was forty-five years old, in April 1859. He was by birth a Vashista Brahmin. Tatya has been described as 'a man of middling stature, with a wheat complexion and always wearing a white chukri-dar turban'. After serving Nana Saheb as an aide-de-camp and commanding officer of a company of sipahis, he became a General when Nana's army was expanded and the conflict widened. Tope had no formal military training, but he seems to have inherited the Maratha genius for guerilla warfare. His talent, and it was a genuine one, as the British learnt in the hardest ways, was for sudden and unexpected moves. He had several of their commanders running around in circles, without the faintest idea of where he was.

The conspicuous part he played in the revolt from May 1857 to April 1859 has in most writings been relegated to the background because of his innate modesty and deep loyalty to Nana. He always professed to act on behalf of the latter. Of his personal life we know little else.

To fit Tatya Tope into context, we will briefly repeat some of the events that have been detailed in the section on Nana Saheb. It will be recollected that the uprising at Kanpur took place on 5 June 1857. Nana Saheb took over the mantle of leading the rebels. The British who were holed up in the entrenchment finally surrendered on 25 June. Two days later they were evacuated to the Satichaura Ghat on the river, and the massacre took place. At the end of June, Nana was installed as Peshwa. General Sir Henry Havelock advanced to Kanpur with a formidable army and Nana opposed him in two battles outside Kanpur. The third battle fought for control of the city was also lost by the rebels and Nana withdrew to Bithur. He then crossed the Ganges and disappeared into Awadh.

At this point, the real initiative passed to Tatya Tope, who from now on acted in Nana's name from Bithur. Havelock, after the recapture of Kanpur, attempted to get to Lucknow but was obstructed en route at each step by the rebels. Tatya Tope, in the meanwhile, was frantically trying to organize the remnants of the troops left at Bithur. After the defeat at Kanpur, many sipahis had disappeared into the countryside or returned to their villages. Tatya's efforts bore fruit and he managed to raise a force of about four thousand men from Nana's remaining troops and the rebel sipahis of some Bengal infantry regiments. He also got hold of two cannons. His aim was to go on building up sufficient strength and then mount another attack on Kanpur. Unfortunately, he did not have enough time for this, because Havelock was back at Kanpur sooner than expected.

Havelock had left James Neill in charge of Kanpur and marched off to Lucknow, but en route he had such heavy casualties that he returned to Kanpur. His fear also was that Tope advancing from Bithur might cut off his lines of communication. Neill, who had been left with a small force at Kanpur and fearing an attack by Tatya, also urged Havelock to return. Thus, on 13 August, Havelock was back, and losing no time, he advanced to Bithur on 16 August.

Tatya Tope had prepared strong defensive positions at Bithur. From behind the breastwork, his massed infantry sent a constant hail of bullets through the British ranks and the two camouflaged cannons, well served by gunners, fired with great precision. The sustained fusillade from Tatya's troops was so severe, and their defensive positions so secure, that Havelock's fourteen heavy guns could make no impression. He was to later comment that not since the Sikh wars had he faced such heavy fire. Havelock then removed part of his European and Sikh troops from the centre front and ordered them to move off into the sugarcane fields on Tatya's flank, and under cover of the plantation, storm the rebel position from that side. This they did successfully, but it involved furious hand-to-hand fighting before the two camouflaged guns were captured and Tatya's men were forced to withdraw.

After this, even clearing the town of Bithur was no easy task for the British as the rebels offered stiff resistance from barricaded houses. Tatya had been defeated but his men had fought bravely and Havelock paid a well-deserved tribute to him. He wrote in his Despatch dated 17 August, 'I must do the mutineers the justice to pronounce that they fought obstinately; otherwise they could not have held their own, even with much advantages of ground, against my powerful artillery fire.'

Despite the fact that his master, Nana, had departed from the scene and he had also been recently defeated at Bithur and his army dispersed, Tatya did not sit licking his wounds. His tenacity, of which we see ample evidence later, was incredible. His first thought was how he would continue this war. For this he needed an army; not just any army; but a trained army, a stronger army, not only in numbers but also in artillery and equipment. With this he could recapture Kanpur, which was at the heart of British communications between Calcutta and Lucknow. As he sat thinking, he suddenly realized that this need not be a pipe dream. He thought of the Gwalior army in which there was simmering discontent. If he could win over to his side the redoubtable Gwalior Contingent and Scindia's 10,000 strong army, it would add enormously to the strength of his own army.

Maharaja Scindia had remained steadfast in his loyalty to the British government, as he felt that his best interests were served by this strategy. This, as mentioned elsewhere, was a great loss for the rebel cause, as Scindia had one of the best trained armies in India. He had also kept his troops loyal by giving them liberal allowances. Those who were inclined towards the nationalist cause, and many were kept happy by vague promises that, if and when the opportunity arose, he would rise against the British.

Scindia's position was, however, rendered difficult when on 31 July, a large number of Holkar's troops from Indore and Indian sipahis from British regiments in Mhow arrived Gwalior after mutinying. The presence of such a large rebel force at Gwalior created much tension for the maharaja, as his own troops were carried away by fervour and they demanded that the maharaja should lead them to Delhi. Scindia took a shrewd stand saying that the Holkar forces and the mutineers from Mhow should go to Delhi, while he would lead the Scindia troops to the capital once the rainy season was over and the traditional campaigning season started.

It was at this stage that Tatya Tope came to Gwalior. He already had contacts in the state forces and these he exploited to the full. He held many parleys with the sipahis and tried to further arouse the rebel impulse that had been kindled by the arrival of the rebel forces from central India. Tatya succeeded in winning over the Gwalior contingent, which in turn made a final effort to win over the maharaja to his side, but the latter remained adamant and clung to the British. Scindia then held a grand parade of all his troops on 8 September and made a stirring appeal to his Maratha troops to dissuade the Gwalior contingent, consisting mainly of 'Hindustani' sipahis from defecting. The appeal went home and the Maratha troops swore loyalty to Scindia, but they could not stop the Gwalior contingent from going Tatya's way. Thus, Tatya was only partially successful in his mission but it was still an important gain as the Gwalior contingent played a prominent role in subsequent events. From almost nothing, Tatya had a ready-made army motivated by a fierce desire to oust the British.

Now a few months later, in the winter of 1857-58, Tatya Tope reappeared once again at Kanpur. This time, in addition to the troops from the rebel headquarters at Kalpi, he had the support of the Gwalior contingent as well as the redoubtable Raja Kunwar Singh and his regiments from Bihar.

By now, Delhi had already fallen to the enemy and other areas of the north had been pacified. As mentioned elsewhere, British Indian regiments from north India had been diverted to Lucknow and Kanpur. Large reinforcements had been received from Britain and other overseas locations. Thus, hugely strengthened, the commander-in-chief's priority was the relief of Lucknow. He marched from Kanpur to the besieged city on 9 November 1857.

For the defense of Kanpur and the vital bridge of boats that connected the town with Lucknow, he left behind a small force of Europeans and Sikhs supported by artillery under General Windham. To strengthen this force, Windham detained some troops who were on their way to Lucknow. He was somewhat later also joined by a Rifle Brigade that had arrived from Fatehpur.

On the day General Campbell advanced with his army towards Lucknow, Tatya Tope moved with his forces from Kalpi to Kanpur, a distance of 70 kilometres. His combined forces clearly outnumbered Windham's. As Tatya closed in on the city, Windham thought he could better defend it and the bridge of boats by moving forward and attacking Tatya's advance guard, with the idea that having inflicted some damage, he would quickly withdraw to his camp. This was a rash move, because Tatya's main body of troops was not far off and as soon as Windhan engaged the advance guard, the main forces moved into the attack. The British suffered heavy casualties and beat a hasty retreat to Kanpur. The next morning, on 27 November, Tatya deployed his troops around enemy positions and started with a heavy cannonade. Windham held his position for five hours but as soon as his front cracked, Tatya unleashed his infantry and the cavalry. Windham's camp was overwhelmed and the Gwalior Contingent occupied all the commanding positions in the city. Windham's position was precarious and he ordered the whole force to fall back into the entrenchment along with stores and guns. But his troops were seized with panic and retreated 'without any semblance of order'.

Rev. Moore, a captain in the army, wrote to his brother about:

> the jolly good licking we have received from our friends in Gwalior. They came down in fine style and commenced the favourite game of long bowls which I regret to say General Windham answered with small guns..... We tried the bowling game until our new Regiment got into a regular funk. An order was now given to spike guns and return, no enemy being up to then in sight. Cavalry, however, charging the gunners advanced by the naval brigade who retreated to such purpose that no three men were to be found together when our Infantry advanced to retaliate the guns. The 88th who had charged the day before refused to advance ... it was a case of save who can. The troops bolted in through the city any way they could and our whole camp fell back into the hands of the enemy, and only if they had followed it up they could have taken the entrenchment, I believe, for we had hardly a man in place fit for duty...

Another document (Br. Museum, Addl. Mss. 37151) graphically details the scene of total chaos in the entrenchment:

> For the entrenchment the scenes of confusion baffle description. In the outside hospital, poor fellows whose legs were only amputated the night before sprang out of bed in agony of fear and it was not until 10 o'clock that anything like order was restored. In the meantime the troops broke open every place for drinks; private stores and baggage were looted; even the hospital comforts were broken open and carried off. The commissariat stores were robbed and in fact the whole place was a scene of the direst confusion and drunkenness. If the enemy had come on that night, I fancy that few men were sober enough to fight. The only exception I know of was the 64th.

Tatya Tope had Kanpur at his mercy. It was a signal victory and as night enveloped the city, he was exultant in his camp and dreaming of re-establishing Nana's authority in Kanpur. Fate, however, willed otherwise; his victory was short lived.

Colin Campbell had left Kanpur on 9 November and after fierce fighting had managed to reach the Lucknow Residency, where some 1,500 men, women and children had been besieged by nationalist troops. Having accomplished this, General Campbell was nervous about Windham's position at Kanpur. One course for him was to first clear Lucknow of all rebel forces, but this would have taken time and Kanpur would have been lost. Tatya's thrust into Kanpur and the possibility of the bridge of boats being destroyed alarmed him and determined his actions. He therefore left a strong movable force outside Lucknow to keep a check on rebel forces, and on 27 November, he marched back to Kanpur with a strong army and encamped six kilometres from the city. He was deeply relieved to find the bridge of boats still intact. Had Tatya destroyed it, Campbell could not have returned and Tatya's victory could have had far-reaching consequences. It still remains a mystery why Tatya did not bring forward his heavy guns and destroy the bridge. His troops had seen heavy fighting throughout the day and were tired and it is possible that Tatya had this planned for the next morning. He obviously miscalculated for he never got the chance. It was a major tactical mistake.

The next day, 29 November, Tatya Tope ordered his heavy guns to be positioned so as to bombard the bridge. Intense fire was opened, but Campbell, equally alive to the importance of saving the bridge replied strongly with his artillery. After a short but sharp artillery duel, the British guns proved superior. Tatya kept firing, but the shots fell on either side of the bridge and did not strike it. Despite facing heavy cannon and musketry fire, Campbell crossed the bridge, thus accomplishing a difficult military operation. At one stage, Tatya also attempted to burn the boat bridge by floating fire rafts down the stream, but this attempt was thwarted by the naval brigade.

Now Campbell approached Kanpur and the two well-matched armies faced each other on 6 December. Tatya Tope's strategy was governed by one major consideration; he did not want to stake his entire army on the fortunes of a single battle. He wanted to engage the enemy in such a manner that, if there was the possibility of defeat, he would be able to extricate his army out of an untenable position. He thus formed his men into two separate bodies with some distance between them. Interspersed were areas of the city of Kanpur. The two separate bodies of troops had their own lines of retreat. It is unnecessary to go into the details of the battle, but broadly, Campbell, like the astute general that he was, took advantage of Tatya's faulty positioning of his troops. He fell with full force on one of the two separate bodies and defeated it before help could come from the other. He then launched a powerful attack against the second body of men. All through the battle, artillery came much into play. Tatya Tope thus lost the battle for Kanpur, but he had the satisfaction of knowing that almost his entire army escaped from the battlefield without significant losses in men; only the baggage and guns fell into British hands.

By the end of 1857, the tide had turned and the British were re-establishing their hold on the country. Despite the setbacks all over north India, it must be said to the credit of the rebel leaders that they continued their struggle with great determination and unshakeable faith.

After his defeat at Kanpur, Tatya Tope returned with his army to Kalpi. Kalpi was the last stronghold of the rebels and was an arsenal containing large quantities of ammunition, guns, mortars, shots and shells. It had factories for the manufacture of cannons and shells and for the repair of arms. There was a subterranean storehouse containing vast quantities of gunpowder, warlike stores, and muskets.

After the British had reconquered north India, they could afford to turn their attention to the last centres of the revolt, which were in central India and Jhansi in particular.

It will be recollected that the British had annexed the state of Jhansi, but Rani Lakshmi Bai had refused to accept their sovereignty and had taken up arms against them. By now the British were in a much stronger position with men and equipment. A lot of time and effort was spent by them in order to assemble the Central India Field Force at Mhow and Sehore that contained seasoned troops, rushed from Britain, and hand-picked Indian troops. This was a considerable force and its strongest arm was the artillery, which would be most effective against the strength of the Jhansi fortifications. The force was accompanied by a siege train established from Bombay. It was further reinforced by the Hyderabad contingent, which, interestingly, was recruited mainly from the Purabia Hindus and Muslims from Awadh who, having been isolated from north India, had not joined their comrades in the mutiny.

Lord Charles John Canning, who considered the Rani as 'the Jezebel of India', was determined to demolish the last areas of the revolt and he selected a seasoned general to head the field force. This man was Sir Hugh Rose, who was one of the most distinguished generals of the British army. He later became a Field Marshal and was elevated to the peerage as Lord Straitnairn. He had varied military and diplomatic experience. He had served in Syria during the Turko-Egyptian war and subsequently served in the Crimean war. By now, Rose was fifty-seven years old but was still a formidable adversary, supported by a strong and experienced force.

When Rose approached Jhansi with the Central India Field Force, Rani Lakshmi Bai sent an appeal to her childhood friends Tatya Tope and Rao Saheb, who were at that time in Kalpi. Tatya responded to such effect that he almost upset British plans. He marched rapidly with a small force of 900 men towards Kalpi and suddenly swooped on the rajas of Panna and Charkhari, who were two important rulers of Bundelkhand. Both were also staunch and unwavering allies of the British.

This put Lord Canning, the governor general, in a quandary. Not to go to the assistance of his allies would be considered an act of betrayal by other princes and might encourage them to rise against the British. He therefore ordered Rose to march at once to the relief of Charkhari. General Rose, however, in conjunction with the agent to the governor general, Sir Robert Hamilton, who was with him at the time, chose to disregard this order. Jhansi was at that point only 14 kilometres away, while Charkhari was 130 kilometres. It appeared to Rose and Hamilton that the surest way to save the less important and more distant place was to attack and capture the more important and nearer fortress of Jhansi.

Meanwhile, Tatya fought his way into the fortress of Charkhari. In the process, he had a windfall in the shape of 24 cannons, which he also captured. In addition, he succeeded in extracting 3 lakh rupees from the maharaja, all of which was very useful for the rebels. Unfortunately Tatya Tope than marched back to Kalpi and left Rose to proceed unhampered to Jhansi. This was a mistake.

Sir Hugh Rose arrived at Jhansi with his army on 20 March 1858. A proven general, Rose was pitted against a young woman, who had no experience of modern warfare. The siege of Jhansi went on day after day. During this time, Rose employed huge siege guns, 24 pounders (mortars) and howitzers to cannonade the fort. Some walls were breached but they were repaired at night. Cannon balls heated red before firing had caused many fires and devastated the city. The Rani's gunners answered back, shot after shot.

By the eleventh day of the siege, the continuous bombardment was taking its toll. The fortunes of Jhansi were on the wane. Rani Lakshmi Bai was deeply worried that her friend Tatya had not come to her help and anxiously scanning the horizon for his approaching army. She had almost despaired of help ever arriving, when on the evening of 31 March 1858, the lookouts glimpsed Tatya Tope's army approaching the Betwa river. That evening, the people of Jhansi saw a huge bonfire that Tatya had set on the hill as a signal of his arrival.

The Rani responded by firing salutes from all the batteries of the fort and the city. On receiving Lakshmi Bai's appeal, Tatya marched out again towards Jhansi. Although his force numbered 15,000 men, a majority of them were raw recruits, with hardly any training.

Rose had set up a telegraph post on one of the hills east of Jhansi and was alerted well in advance that Tatya Tope was approaching. His position was perilous. Before him was Jhansi, an unconquered fortress garrisoned by warriors full of the ardour of battle and close to him was an army led by a chieftain who had recently revelled in defeating the English. But Rose faced it with his usual daring. He had to decide whether to withdraw his troops from the investment of Jhansi to meet Tatya, or confront him with only a part of his force while the siege continued uninterrupted. He chose the latter course. Rose detached the men who were to face Tatya and drew them up in two columns during the might with the intention of attacking at daybreak. But Tatya forestalled him by advancing before daybreak on a broad front. Both sides then opened with heavy artillery and musketry fire along the entire front. The British fire had little effect, especially as Tatya Tope's line overlapped the British on both flanks. Rose therefore massed his horse artillery and cavalry on the right and the left and attacked both the flanks of Tatya's line. The rebel army's only well-trained troops were the rebel sipahis and the Afghan mercenaries, who met the charge most bravely. They were, however, handicapped by their slow-firing matchlocks and in Rose's own words, 'The enemy poured a fusillade into the cavalry; the sipahis jumped up in hundreds on high rocks and boulders to load and fire but before they could reload their matchlocks, Capt. Need leading his troops in advance penetrated into the midst of them. The attack on the enemy's right was equally successful and they broke and they retired in confusion.' Although groups of sipahis and Afghans stood fast and fought it out to the last, this made little difference.

The British then advanced with infantry and artillery on Tatya's second line, which occupied the rising ground covered with jungle and was commanded by Tatya Tope in person. He saw with dismay his inexperienced men from the flanks rushing back towards him and causing utter confusion. As a result, Tatya's second line could not hold either. He realized the day was lost, but there was a chance of saving his guns. He at once set fire to the dry jungle and under cover of the smoke and flames he retreated across the Betwa river. He lost several of his guns and much ammunition, but most of his army managed to retire to Kalpi.

The battle of Betwa was a disaster, an ignominious defeat. Even accepting that Tatya Tope's troops were untrained and equipped with the outdated matchlocks, the fact was that his forces vastly outnumbered the enemy. Individually, his troops fought bravely and British eyewitness accounts acknowledge that 'not a man asked for quarter'. Therefore, the defeat can be ascribed to Tatya's faulty tactics.

But, for this failure of Tatya Tope, the Rani was also partly responsible. The Jhansi force could have sallied out and fallen on the depleted army that had been left behind by Rose to continue the siege, while the battle at the Betwa was raging furiously. A double attack, one led by Tatya and the other by the Rani may have yielded a spectacular result. The Rani missed out on this initiative. It is believed that she was constrained from this course of action by a traitor in her camp, who as we see later, did her down.

After the battle of Betwa, Tatya returned to Kalpi where Rao Saheb was encamped with the rebel army. About this time, Rao Saheb had assumed the title of Peshwa. Meanwhile, Rani Lakshmi Bai fought on at Jhansi, but after the continuous bombardment lasting fourteen days, the walls of the fort were breached and Rose's troops entered the fort. The Rani led her men in a hand-to-hand fight and killed many of the enemies herself. But, finally, the British took control and she had to escape from the fort. After an incredible 24-hour ride, during which she was pursued by Rose's men, she arrived at Kalpi to join Rao Saheb and Tatya Tope. (*See* Ch. six for a detailed account).

Present at this time in Kalpi were the old allies: Mardan Singh the Raja of Banpur; the Raja of Shahgarh; other rebel rajas and several of the Rani's soldiers. The troops at Kalpi were composed of diverse groups who had gathered under one flag and had a common objective. They included some regiments of the rebel Gwalior State army, several rebel battalions who had served in the British forces, the Kotah cavalry, troops of the rebel rajas and the remnants of the Jhansi force. Half the number were composed of ill-trained peasants and camp followers, who were more interested in plunder than actual fighting.

Sir Hugh Rose meanwhile allowed time to his men for rest and recuperation. He also appealed to the commander-in-chief for reinforcements and was joined by a brigade of highlanders. It was now early May and the European troops suffered severely from the heat. The powerful sun compelled Rose to march at night; even so, there were a number of fatalities from sunstroke.

Meanwhile, at Kalpi, there was much reorganization of the rebel army, to which both Tatya and Lakshmi Bai contributed. After much discussion, Rao Saheb appointed Tatya as the commander of the army. Lakshmi Bai, who had a real flair for leadership, was seriously considered but it was unheard of for a woman to lead an army. She, however, worked closely with Tatya Tope and continued to exercise much influence in the planning.

It was felt that Rao Saheb's army must not bottle itself within the walls of Kalpi, where superior British artillery would tilt the scales, as had happened at Jhansi. It was therefore decided that the Peshwa's army should go forward 70 kilometres towards Jhansi and meet the enemy on favourable ground at the town of Kunch. This site offered several defensive advantages as it was difficult to approach, surrounded by temples and woods and protected by high mud walls.

At Kunch, Tatya made a mistake in committing too many of his troops to the centre, blocking the obvious and direct route from Jhansi. He did not keep adequate troops in reserve, in case Rose should attempt to turn one or the other flank. This became evident as soon as the battle of Kunch began.

As Rose approached Kunch, it was precisely a flank attack that he opted for. He made a flank march with his whole force to the north-west of Kunch. This position also seriously threatened Tatya's line of retreat to Kalpi and exposed the north-west of Kunch, which was not protected by entrenchments. A three-pronged attack by Rose's army followed with the huge siege guns directing their fire on the town. The flank attack caused the rebels to draw back, but for a time, Major Orr commanding the Hyderabad contingent, was pushed back by a counter attack of musket fire and Maratha swords. But the well-trained Indian sipahis of the British forces forged ahead despite heavy rebel artillery and musketry fire. The battle was a short one and Tatya's army was defeated. The only credit that can be given to the rebels was that the retreat was disciplined. Sir John Kaye's description is interesting:

> Then was witnessed action on the part of the rebels which impelled admiration from their enemies. The manner in which they conducted the retreat could not be surpassed. They remembered the lessons which their European officers had well taught them. There was no hurry, no disorder, no rushing to the rear. All was orderly as on field day. Though their line of skirmishers was two miles in length, it never wavered in a single point. The men fired, then ran behind the relieving men and loaded. The relieving men then fired and ran back in turn. They even attempted, when they thought the pursuit was too rash, to take up position, so as to bring on it an enfilading fire.

A British officer who was present is quoted in the report of the Intelligence Branch of Army Headquarters as saying that when the retreating rebels were charged, they threw aside their muskets and fought desperately with their *talwars*. His comments give a clear account of the hand-to-hand combat of the time and the excellence of the Indian *talwar* as a fighting weapon.

The British were, however, unable to capitalize on this victory as they were too exhausted to keep up the pursuit, and Tatya Tope's army was able to withdraw to Kalpi. Although English casualties were few in the actual fighting, the numbers struck down by heat and exhaustion were considerable. Interestingly, Tatya was aware that the foreigners were suffering intensely from the heat and had ordered his commanders not to attack before 10 o'clock in the morning, as fighting in the heat of the midday sun would finish them off faster at least or send them to hospital.

Rose wrote three days later that he would have achieved a real victory 'had not the dreadful heat paralysed the men ... I was obliged four times to get off my horse by excessive debility. The doctor poured cold water over me, and gave restoratives, which enabled me to go on again. I do not think I shall stay in India to pass such another torment as 100 in the shade'.

There are several references both in British and Indian sources to the difficulties the white soldiers faced due to the physical hardships of the long marches and their prostration and exhaustion due to the summer heat. At the subsequent battle against Tatya at Kotah-ki-Serai, British soldiers fell off from their saddles due to the intense heat and had to be replaced by the *Purabia* sipahis.

The defeat at Kunch led to various recriminations among the Peshwa's army. The infantry taunted the cavalry for having abandoned them, and the cavalry blamed the gunners. Tatya Tope was also accused of using faulty tactics. At Kalpi, where the army had fled, there was despair and gloom.

After the battle, Tatya Tope went to the village of Charkhi, 6 kilometres from Jalaun, where his parents lived. His future was so uncertain that he wanted a last meeting with them. From there he slipped away in disguise to Gwalior on the important mission of once again trying to win over Maharaja Scindia's 10,000-men army. On the last visit he had succeeded in detaching the Gwalior contingent from Scindia, and they had marched off with Tatya to Kalpi. However, the Scindia army, consisting mainly of Marathas, had remained loyal to the Maharaja. On the current visit, Tatya Tope was able to shake the loyalty of the army and many of the soldiers were inclined to join the rebel cause. The situation, however, remained on edge.

While Tatya was away at Gwalior, he missed the battle at Kalpi where Rao Saheb and Rani Lakshmi Bai were caught in a life and death struggle. This battle has been described in detail in chapter six but a brief recapitulation is necessary here.

As mentioned, Kalpi was the last stronghold of the rebels. There were extensive ravines around the town and the Peshwa's army made good use of the topography. But Rose's spies had done some good work and apprised Rose of the rebel plan of a feint through the ravines under Rao Saheb, with the main attack coming on the right wing. On this wing, the Rani, in person, at the head of the Red Cavalry charged through the British line, getting within a few yards of the British field guns and sabring the gunners. But Rose was a canny general, among the best. When he saw the collapse, he swiftly brought up the Sikh Camel Corps, which he had kept in reserve as a reinforcement. The two sides were then locked in close combat, but gradually the rebel stranglehold was loosened and both, Rao Saheb in the ravines and the Rani on the wing, were pushed back. Another battle had been lost.

Kalpi fell the next day. The morale of the rebels had been broken and there was no resistance. The British thought that the campaign had now been completed and the commander-in-chief, Sir Colin Campbell, decided that the Central India Field Force should be broken up and distributed. Rose issued a farewell proclamation to his troops and congratulated them on 'having marched more than a thousand miles and having taken more than a hundred guns'. But before Rose could actually leave, the most shattering news arrived at the headquarters. This news, said a Calcutta newspaper, 'caused throughout India a sensation hardly less than that caused by the news of the outbreak of the mutiny'.

From Kalpi, Rani Lakshmi Bai and Rao Saheb had fled to Gopalpur, 80 kilometres from Gwalior. Here they were joined by the Nawab of Banda and Tatya Tope. The latter had missed the battle of Kalpi and had gone to Gwalior with the object of winning over the army. At Kalpi, the rebels had suffered disastrous losses; they had no cannons, no equipment and only the remains of an army, whose morale was poor. The sipahis wanted to go back to Awadh, while Rao Saheb thought that their best chance lay in the Deccan, which was once the heartland of the Maratha empire. If they could march south and unfurl the standard of the Peshwa in the Deccan, thousands of Marathas would flock to it. The Holkars of Indore would also join. The British had denuded this region of troops, which had been rushed north for the rebellion. But the Deccan was a 1000 kilometres away.

It was then that the Rani electrified the assembled leaders by making a startling suggestion. She said that Tatya Tope had half won over the Scindia army and undermined the Maharaja. 'Let us not just win over the army,' she said, 'but let us capture the capital city of Gwalior, with its impregnable fort. We will acquire not only military strength, but also great political influence. We can start anew, we can fight the British again.' It was a daring and original suggestion and could have serious repercussions for the enemy.

This suggestion, it was also thought, came from Tatya Tope and not the Rani, but the historians Sir John Kaye and Colonel Malleson write:

> The situation seemed desperate to the rebel chieftains. But desperate situations suggest desperate remedies; a remedy which, on first inspection, might well seem desperate, did occur to the fertile brain of one of the confederates. To which one is not certainly known. But, judging the leading group of conspirators by their antecedents – Rao Saheb, the Nawab of Banda, Tatya Tope and the Rani of Jhansi – we may at once dismiss the first two from consideration. They possessed neither the character nor the genius to conceive a plan so vast and so daring. Of the two who remain, we may dismiss Tatya Tope. Not that he was incapable of forming the design, but ... we have his statement and in that he takes to himself no credit for the most successful act with which his career is associated. The fourth conspirator possessed the genius, the daring, the despair necessary for the conception of great deeds. She was urged on by hatred, by desire of vengeance .... The conjecture, then amounts to certainty that the desperate remedy which the confederates decided to execute at Gopalpur was suggested and pressed upon his comrades by the daring Rani of Jhansi.

The scheme was acted upon immediately. The leaders could recognize the possibilities before them and even hope that if the first blow was successful, the fortunes of the campaign might change. Tatya's close links with Gwalior had enabled him to win over the Gwalior contingent and this unit had fought under him in earlier battles, in one of which he had routed the British. During his second visit, Tatya had half convinced Scindia's army, but their defection was still uncertain.

The Gwalior fort, built in 950 AD by a Rajput chieftain, stands on a rocky hill which rises above the surrounding country. The main entrance to the fort is through a steep path defended by five gateways placed at strategic points along its course. It is one of the most formidable forts in India.

Maharaja Jiyajee Rao Scindia was completely loyal to the British, although he did not like them personally. He was the most important of the Maratha chiefs and wielded great influence all over central and western India. Had he joined the rebels in the earlier stages of the rebellion, the story of 1857-58 might well have been different. As Malleson says, 'For four months Scindia had probably the fate of India in his hands. Had he revolted in June, the siege of Delhi must have been raised, Agra and Lukhnow would have fallen; it is more than probable that Punjab would have risen.'

The young maharaja was greatly influenced by his shrewd chief minister, Dinkar Rao Rajwade. The British Resident at Gwalior, Major Macpherson, had already fled to Agra for safety. The reasoning at Gwalior was that if they joined the rebellion, the English could be confined to Bengal, but what would happen to Gwalior? There would be many contenders for supremacy. The emperor at Delhi, with the help of the sipahis, could become supreme or the Sikhs of the Punjab, or Nana Saheb or even Holkar. Scindia refused to take those risks and preferred servitude. The people of Gwalior and the army, however, thought differently. Within living memory, their people, the Marathas, had dominated India, and the emperor at Delhi was a puppet in their hands. In their eyes, the maharaja was playing a doubtful role, for he owed his principality to the Peshwa and it was his duty to rally around Nana Saheb instead of supporting the hated foreigners. Gwalior was therefore ripe for the picking and Tatya Tope on his visit found much sympathy for the rebel cause, as he reported on his return to Gopalpur.

Rao Saheb and the others thought that with the ground work done by Tatya, they would be able to enter without firing a shot. Rao Saheb wrote to Maharaja Scindia that he did not wish to interfere with the state's administration but he did want money and provisions for his army and an unopposed passage through Gwalior territories on his way to the Deccan, the land of promise. He also said the people of Gwalior were against the British and sympathized with the rebel cause.

Maharaja Scindia had, however, been told that the rebel army was broken down and was in the last stages of destitution and one volley would suffice to disperse them. He was young and impulsive, and wanted to show his loyalty to his British masters, but he had not inherited the genius of his warlike ancestors and his followers had no sympathy for the cause he represented. Dinkar Rao had advised him either to await British reinforcements or meet the insurgents attack from behind the strong ramparts of the Gwalior fort.

Scindia ignored the advice and on 1 June marched out with about 8,000 men and several guns and took up a position about two miles east of the rebels at Morar. Scindia's guns opened fire on the Peshwa's forces, which was totally unexpected by the Peshwa. For a while they thought that the volley was really a salute of welcome, till the shells started falling close. The Rani at the head of 2,000 cavalry advanced towards the guns. The smoke of the discharge from Scindia's cannons had scarcely disappeared when the 2,000 horsemen charging at a gallop, carried the guns. Immediately after, the rebels raised a loud cry of '*deen, deen*'. Scindia's troops responded in the same manner, and fraternized with the Peshwa's army. Many went off to eat watermelons in the bed of the Morar river, which was very sensible considering the searing heat of June. It was obvious by the reactions of Scindia's troops, that Tatya Tope's efforts to soften the Gwalior army had indeed worked. They had joined the revolt.

The maharaja's bodyguard put up a brave struggle and many of them were killed. Scindia then fled from the field and did not draw the reins till he reached the safety of Agra. He even left his rani and his seraglio behind, who were treated very courteously by the rebels and given shelter in the Narwar fortress nearby.

The first part of the rebel plan had succeeded admirably; Rao Saheb and his army entered Gwalior in triumph. They took the treasury and Scindia's jewels, the latter said to be of fabulous value. With the money, the rebel leaders paid Scindia's army and their own men several months' wages. Strict orders were also issued that there must not be any looting. However, the maharaja's old palace, the British Residency, Dinkar Rao Rajwade's mansion and also those of other *sardars* (noblemen) who were sympathetic to the British were burnt to the ground.

The capture of Gwalior was an extremely important development for the rebels. They had acquired the impregnable fort of Gwalior and also a well-trained army and strong artillery. After Kalpi they were a helpless lot, but now they were not only a military power but also a political power. If they could arrange the defence of Gwalior and march south to the Deccan, where there were powerful Maratha states still loyal to their former government, the situation could change again and the British could face disaster once again.

Tantya Tope was proclaimed as the Peshwa and Rao Saheb as the governor of Gwalior. To celebrate the fall of Gwalior, Rao Saheb held a grand durbar and feast at the fort. At the festivities, Tatya Tope was accorded special precedence. The celebrations, rather stupidly, went on for several days, almost as if liberation from the hated British had already been achieved. The more realistic among the leaders, like the Rani and Tatya Tope, felt that time was being wasted on trivialities and celebrations were being held before victory had been won. They urged that preparations for war must be immediately made; that the strength and the resources of the British must not be underestimated. They would soon advance to Gwalior. The control of Scindia's army, his fort and his fabulous treasury was a God-sent opportunity and it should not be frittered away. The Rani and Tatya exhorted Rao Saheb to organize the defence of the city and put the soldiers under capable commanders who would motivate them and bring them to peak fighting fitness.

Possibly, Rao Saheb was not being altogether foolish. All these impressive ceremonies had propaganda value. He was creating a new rallying point for the rebels all over the country and believed that the princes of the Deccan would rise in a body and rally around him. But Tatya and the Rani, both realists, thought that without victory all this was a vain and empty show. Tatya Tope's and the Rani's remonstrations had some effect because, finally, Rao Saheb decided to strengthen the defence of Gwalior. Letters were dispatched to rebel rajas still in the district, notably, Raja Mardan Singh of Banpur and the Raja of Shahgarh, who had earlier fought valiantly against the British. They were invited to join the government at Gwalior. The command of the troops encamped outside the city was entrusted to the Rani of Jhansi, while those within Gwalior were entrusted to Tatya Tope. Four Maratha noblemen who had helped the rebels and had been imprisoned by the maharaja were released and honoured and thereafter sent to the districts to raise troops to oppose the British. But Rao Saheb had left all this far too late and when Rose arrived, he was unprepared for the British attack.

The news of the fall of Gwalior reached Sir Hugh Rose on 4 June at Kalpi. He was stunned at the audacious move of the rebels and fully realized the danger of the situation. The monsoon was imminent and the land would be untraversable by guns and heavy equipment and the rivers would be in flood. It was the least favourable time for military operations. Further, the delay would give the rebels time to recruit more princes and men to their banner and the rebellion could assume dangerous proportions.

Sir Colin Campbell, the commander-in-chief, now had troops to spare as the revolt had been suppressed in most parts of the country. He sent reinforcements to Rose once again. Colonel Riddell, who was with his force north of the Jumna, was ordered to join Rose. A brigade of the Rajputana field force under Brigadier Smith was also despatched to Gwalior. The Hydrabad contingent, who were in the process of returning home, were ordered instead to Gwalior. Rose ordered all units to move into position.

Three battles were fought for Gwalior. A detailed account of these would be tedious. Eight kilometres to the east of Gwalior is the Morar cantonment, which was held in strength by Tatya's troops. Rose commanded the British force here in person. The battle for Morar was fiercely contested and Tatya's men fought for every inch. Casualties on both sides were heavy. After several hours of fighting, Rose captured Morar.

Kotah-ki-Sarai is 10 kilometres south-east of Gwalior. Brigadier Smith of the Rajputana Field Force along with the Hyderabad Contingent was positioned to strike here. The Rani was in command of the rebels in this sector. The first day's fighting was inconclusive but Smith had to withdraw rapidly as a body of the Rani's cavalry threatened the baggage of the British Indian troops. The next morning, Smith advanced again and the battle raged fast and furious. The rebels held their ground and the Rani led her troops to repeated attacks, but her ranks were becoming thinner and thinner. She was in the foremost ranks, when suddenly she fell from a carbine shot, mortally wounded. It was only after that the enemy broke through.

Meanwhile, Sir Hugh Rose at Morar was planning a strike on Gwalior. He realized that his force could not cross the plain between Morar and Gwalior as it would come under fire from the formidable batteries of the fort. He therefore made a wide detour but this necessitated the construction of a bridge across a canal by the Madras Sappers. Tatya's gunners made the task very difficult. As Tatya was preparing to launch an attack east of the canal, Rose counter-attacked with mass infantry and heavy artillery support. Out numbered and out-gunned, Tatya had to retire. After this, he could not hold Gwalior for long as British troops had occupied the heights that commanded the plain. Thus on 19 June, Gwalior fell.

By mid-1858 the war had almost been won by the British. The rebel strongholds in United Provinces and Central India – Delhi, Kanpur, Lucknow, Jhansi, Kalpi, Bareilly, and Gwalior – had fallen one by one. Yet, when the hope of success had all but vanished, the war was prolonged by almost a year by the remarkable guerilla warfare and grim determination of Tatya Tope, as well as by the heroic resistance of the people of Awadh.

After the British reoccupied Gwalior and the Rani of Jhansi was dead, there still remained Tatya Tope and Rao Saheb. The British troops caught up with the retreating Tatya Tope at Jawra Alipur, a few miles from Gwalior. Tatya's remaining men put up a fight but were defeated and, much to the chagrin of the British, both Tatya and Rao Saheb escaped.

The British then decided that the revolt was over. The Central India Field Force was disbanded and Sir Hugh Rose left for England. Everyone thought that it was now time to relax and recover from the trauma of the past one and a half years. But the revolt had not ended. Tatya Tope had disappeared only to return. Within a few weeks of his latest defeat, the jungles of central India and the semi-arid districts of Rajputana (present-day Rajasthan) were echoing with the name and deeds of this brave rebel.

The British set up a cordon of their troops in both these areas. But Tatya led these forces a real dance. W.H. Russel, a correspondent with the *Times,* wrote graphically in January 1859:

> Our remarkable friend, Tatya Tope, is too troublesome and clever an enemy to be admired. Since June last he has kept central India in fervour. He has sacked stations, plundered treasuries, emptied arsenals, collected armies, lost them; fought battles, lost them; taken guns from native princes, lost them, taken more, lost them; then his motions have been like forked lightining; for weeks he has marched thirty and forty miles a day. He has crossed the Nurbudda to and fro; he has marched between our columns behind them and before them. Ariel was not more subtly aided by the best stage mechanisms. Up mountains, over rivers, through ravines and valleys, amid swamps, on he goes, backwards and forward, and sideways and zigzag ways now falling upon a post cart and carrying off the Bombay mails – now looting a village … and burned yet evasive as Proteus.

Tatya quickly realized that the time for pitched battles was over and he now concentrated on guerilla warfare – and a marvelous guerilla warrior he made. He knew that the war was almost over, the tide was running with the British and, consequently, he could no longer count on the active support of the civil population, yet this last rebel fought on. His dedication and fervour are beyond comparison.

During the time that Tatya continued his war, Rao Saheb was with him. After Jawra Alipur, where Tatya and Rao Saheb had last faced the British, the two turned to Rajputana, where there were a large number of princely states and people with a long tradition of warfare. Tatya believed that although they could not now arouse sentiment for their cause in the populace, they might be able to assure their neutrality. He was also certain that he could persuade the troops of the princely states to take up arms against the British. Tatya had also written a letter to all the nobles of Jaipur, inviting them to join him. The British heard of this letter and immediately sent the Rajputana Field Force after him to Jaipur. Tatya moved southwards to the small state of Tonk, where the Nawab shut himself up in his fort, while his army joined Tatya's force. Thus reinforced, he marched to Bundi, but the ruler closed the gates of the town in his face. He wasted no time in besieging Bundi as a British flying column under Colonel Holmes was in pursuit. Tatya then made it known publicly that he was moving to southern Rajputana, but in fact he turned west to an area of the Banas river between Nasirabad and Neemuch, where the spirit of revolt was still alive. General Roberts of the Rajputana Field Force was following, but was badly bogged down because the rainy season was in full swing. Finally, Roberts caught up with Tatya Tope's force and aware that the flying column under Colonel Holmes was moving up behind Tatya, he decided to attack. Crossing the Banas river, he got his artillery into action against the rebels. During the night, Tatya and his troops disappeared and were next heard of in the Udaipur area.

Robert's Field Force and Holmes's flying column then linked up and their combined force moved after Tatya Tope. They soon made contact with his advance guard and from the prisoners taken the British learnt that the main rebel force was at the Banas river, some 10 kilometres away. Tatya, meanwhile, heard from his spies that the enemy was advancing. He had a naturally strong position, with the river in front of him. The river also protected him from the right, and to the left lay steep hills. Across the river was a flat plain that offered no cover to the enemy. So Tatya thought that despite the small number of troops under his command, he might give the enemy a fight. When the British arrived, Tatya Tope's four guns opened heavy fire. Despite suffering casualties, the Indian sipahis under British command forded the river and scaled the hill, while their cavalry attacked the centre. This broke Tatya's line and his small force retreated. However, the British pursuit was not fruitful because the rebels reached the jungle, where the cavalry could not operate.

Tatya Tope now headed for the Chambal river with General Roberts in hot pursuit. But near Chittor, Roberts handed the chase over to Brigadier Parke, who had come up from Neemuch to cut off the rebels from the south. Parke believed that Tatya Tope with his men, equipment, and elephants could not cross the mighty Chambal as it was swollen by the monsoon rain; therefore, he followed in a leisurely fashion, only to find that Tatya had crossed the river. Parke looked at the huge, fast-flowing river and gave up the chase and returned to Neemuch.

Tatya Tope moved fast with his troops and arrived at Jhalrapatan in Jhalawar state. Here the state troops welcomed him and the raja was forced to pay a large ransom before he was allowed to get away. At Jhalrapatan, Tatya, who had lost his guns at the Banas river, obtained thirty cannons and horses and other military stores. All these were badly needed. His men also got five days to recuperate in Jhalrapatan as the swollen Chambal blocked pursuit.

Indore was only 80 kilometres from here and a Maratha stronghold. Tatya Tope headed that way with the plan of raising the flag of rebellion there. But the British had also moved fast and hearing of Tatya's direction, General Michel, commanding Malwa, set off in pursuit and despite the heavy monsoon rain caught up with the rebels at Rajgarh. But Michel's men were tired out by the long, fast marches and night was coming in, so it was decided that the attack on Tatya would take place the next morning. But to the surprise of the British as the day dawned, Tatya and his troops, artillery, elephants, and horses had all disappeared – only their tracks remained.

Tatya and his force now melted into the jungle around Sironj. The British tightened the cordon around the area. Brigadier Parke blocked the routes to Indore and Bhopal, Smith's brigade advanced from the north, Colonel Liddell was bearing down from the north-east, while General Michel was marching in from the west.

At this point, while the noose was tightening and Tatya was zig-zagging in the forest country, we need to digress and introduce Raja Maan Singh, who was to later play a calamitous role. Maan Singh was a vassal of the Maharaja of Gwalior, but he was incensed against his overlord because the latter had done him out of some territory from his ancestral state of Narwar. He raised an army and rebelling against the maharaja, captured the fort of Paori, about 150 kilometres south of Gwalior. Smith, who was marching down with his brigade towards Tatya's hideout, was ordered to Paori Fort. Maan Singh sent Smith a message saying that he was not in rebellion against the British but only against the Maharaja. He went on to add, 'I have no connection with Tatya Tope or the rebels and no conflict with the English.' However, the British felt that Maan Singh must be punished for breaking the peace and as Scindia of Gwalior was a close ally, Maan Singh was attacked at Paori. After a heavy bombardment lasting two days, Maan Singh and his troops abandoned the fort and vanished.

It was now the middle of September and Tatya Tope and Rao Saheb emerged from their forest hideouts and, evading the British cordon, plundered a couple of small towns. They then decided to split forces for a while, thus making it easier to evade the enemy. Tatya took a majority of the troops and five guns, while Rao Saheb took six guns but fewer men. Tatya moved towards Chanderi in Bundelkhand. Scindia's forces manned the fort here and Tatya Tope was unable to capture it. While he was busy with this, General Michel caught up with him at Mangrauli on 10 October. Tatya was forced into a fight, but with a stronger force ranged against him, he had little chance and abandoned his guns and fled.

He always remained ahead of his pursuers, stopping now and then to fight them, seemingly defeated, only to reappear somewhere else. The British made prodigious marches to catch up with Tatya, they threw aside their baggage and their tents, they covered 60 kilometres a day, but Tatya did eighty. In the end, the British had to halt and rest.

At the end of October, Tatya joined up with Rao Saheb again. This time they crossed the Narmada river and turned south to Nagpur, a former Maratha state. A year earlier, Tatya Tope would have been received here with joy and he might well have been able to spread the revolt further south into the territory of the Nizam of Hyderabad. Now it was too late and no one was prepared to join a revolt that was faltering and almost dying. He did, however, receive some reinforcements here but was disappointed by the reaction at Nagpur, so he crossed the Narmada again and headed for Baroda, another Maratha state where the embers of rebellion still glowed, although dimly. En route, Parke's troops overtook and defeated his small force.

Tatya Tope and Rao Saheb then turned once again towards Rajputana. At this time, they had only 1,500 men behind them. Not far from Jaipur, Tatya fought the British again and lost more than one tenth of his men. The rest managed to get away, as did Tatya and Rao Saheb. They went south to Mandsaur, but were closely followed by the British. At this time, Tatya Tope was joined by Maan Singh, who on quitting the Paori Fort near Gwalior was still on the run from the British. He brought some troops with him. Feroz Shah, who had fought the British in Rohilkhand, also appeared with his small force in Tatya Tope's camp. Their total strength at the time did not exceed 2,000 men.

Meanwhile, the British trap was closing. It seemed impossible for Tatya and his men to escape. But escape they did. A British force bore down on them at Dausa, near Jaipur, on 14 January 1859. The rebels lost many of their men, but the rest and their leaders got away. They were surprised again at Sikar, north of Jaipur on 21 January, and after a skirmish, once again disappeared.

I quote from Tatya Tope's disposition.

> I had been quarrelling with Rao Saheb all the way, and I told him I could flee no longer, and that whenever I saw an opportunity for doing so, I should leave him. The opportunity for doing so here offered and I left him ... But three men (two Pandits to cook any food and one *Sais*) and three horses and one *tattu* (pony) accompanied me ... We reached the Paron jungle and met Raja Maan Singh. The Raja said, "Why did you leave your force? You have not acted right in doing so." I replied, "I am tired of running away".

Tatya Tope had fought like a tiger, day after day, month after month, and year after year, in battle after battle. But now he was tired; he was giving up.

The British had no idea where Tatya Tope and Rao Saheb were. The locals were hostile to them and they could get no information from them on the rebel leaders. They wanted Tatya badly. Till he was caught or killed, the rebellion would not be over. All their efforts, all the pursuit with large bodies of troops over Central India and Rajputana, all had been in vain. So they decided on a different track; the weak link in Tatya's chain was Maan Singh. He was finding the life of a fugitive pretty rough. Although the British had treated him as a rebel, his real quarrel was with his overlord Maharaja Scindia. They thought that if he was given some support and promises of reconciliation with the maharaja, he might surrender and join the British. Captain Meade, who commanded a cavalry unit, made contact with Maan Singh's agent. Meade promised Maan Singh his life and some help with his confiscated lands. A week later, on 25 March, several members of Maan Singh's party arrived at Meade's camp and after further negotiations it was agreed that Maan Singh would meet Meade, provided he was received with the honour due to a raja, which he was. Meade and Maan Singh met and discussed the situation for two days. Maan Singh felt that he could not betray Tatya Tope unless he got a specific assurance that the territory from his small state would be returned to him. General promises of effecting a reconciliation with the Maharaja were not enough. But ultimately, Maan Singh accepted Meade's promise that his claim, if established, would be 'faithfully considered by the Government'.

Once this was done, the next step was to physically get hold of Tatya Tope. There were spies in Meade's camp, so the whole operation had to be conducted in strict secrecy. If Meade sent a detachment of only Europeans, it would be obvious that something special was afoot. Meade therefore decided to send a party of Indian sipahis under an Indian officer. Tatya's name was never mentioned. The party went on foot; no horses were taken, in case Tatya, hearing them, disappeared into the jungle. The sipahis were hidden, while Maan Singh went on foot alone to meet Tatya. It is a mystery why Tatya trusted Maan Singh so much. They talked till night and then laid down to rest. At about midnight, Tatya Tope went to sleep and Maan Singh brought in the troops. There was a slight struggle during which Tatya's three attendants escaped. The only possessions on Tatya Tope were his sword, a long dagger, three gold armlets, and 118 gold coins.

The British kept a very close watch on Tatya because of the fear that he might escape. In fact, attempts were made by some to bribe the guard. On 15 April, Tatya Tope was brought before a court martial at Shivpuri. Tatya's defense was: 'I have only obeyed in all things I did, my master's [Nana Saheb] orders up to the capture of Kalpi and afterwards those of Rao Saheb. I have nothing to state except that I had nothing to do with the murder of any European men, women or children.' Through the court martial, Tatya Tope, loyal as always, was anxious of absolving not only himself, but also Nana Saheb of the guilt for the two massacres at Kanpur. Interestingly, Tatya Tope was not charged with the murder of British men, women and children in the verdict. As expected, he was sentenced to death by hanging. Tatya Tope only asked that his family should not be punished for anything he had done.

The execution was fixed for four o'clock on the evening of 18 April 1859. Troops surrounded the scaffold and a large audience of his countrymen stood behind them. Tatya Tope mounted the ladder firmly and faced death with complete indifference and tranquility. His last words to the executioners were, 'Finish the job quickly. I want to join eternity without delay.' His body was kept hanging for the remainder of the evening. Those attending made a great scramble to get a lock of his hair.

The rebellion had finally ended for the British. The last rebel was dead.

Malleson pays the following well-deserved tribute to him:

> Tantia Topi was a marvelous guerilla warrior. In pursuit of him, Brigadier Parke had marched, consecutively, 240 miles in nine days; Brigadier Somerset, 230 in nine days, and, again, seventy miles in forty-eight hours: Colonel Holmes, through a sandy desert, fifty-four miles in a little over twenty-four hours; Brigadier Honner, 145 miles in four days. Yet he slipped through them all – through enemies watching every issue of the jungles in which he lay concealed, only to fall at last through the treachery

> of a trusted friend. His capture, and the surrender of Maan Singh, finished the war in central India. Thenceforth his name only survived.

The uniform of Tatya Tope is now preserved in London, in the Royal United Service Museum, Whitehall. It is an *achkan* made of black woollen material, embroidered with *zari*. The inscription reads: 'Coat of the Indian rebel leader, Tantia Topi, who was hanged on 18 April 1859'.

Rao Saheb had remained with Tatya after Gwalior, but some time in 1859, he gave up the fight, became a *sadhu* and renounced the world. He lived in the forests of the Punjab in isolation for four years. Spies of the British, however, discovered his whereabouts and he was captured near Jammu. Although Rao Saheb was in no way involved in the massacre of the English at Kanpur, and an initial enquiry had confirmed this, he had to atone for the deeds of others. The British put up witnesses who obliged the authorities by testifying against Rao Saheb. He was found guilty and was hanged at Bithur in front of his own palace on 2 August 1862. The Nawab of Banda took the easiest way out. He took advantage of the amnesty offered by the British in November 1858 and was rewarded with a pension.

... AND SOME VILLAINS

During the rebellion, there was much brutality on both the sides. While British historians have written volumes about the atrocities of the Indians, most have white-washed the hideous terror unleashed by their own countrymen. Some even stooped so low to proclaim the misdeeds of their own compatriots and even took pride in bragging about them. There were thousands in the British army who were involved in this orgy of murder and rape. The three who exemplify the misdeeds are John Nicholson, William Hodson, and James Neill.

John Nicholson

John Nicholson was a hero for the British and a devil incarnate for the Indians. He was a tall man with a long black beard and a commanding presence. He was in his mid-thirties at the time of the rebellion and had proved himself a dashing soldier in the disastrous British campaign in Afghanistan and in the Sikh wars. In 1857, Nicholson was a lieutenant colonel, but in civil employment and posted as a deputy commissioner at Peshawar.

He was an Irish Protestant and believed that God's finger rested on his shoulder. In reality he was an obscure official known only within his circle, who in a few short weeks was catapulted into the position of a hero by his countrymen. It was a difficult, even a critical time, for the British and they needed heroes after the bungling and the blunders they had made, which led to the uprising, giving them the fright of their collective lives.

When news of the rebellion reached Peshawar in mid-May 1857, Nicholson and his superior took swift action. The Indian sipahis were disarmed and their leaders executed. Whole regiments were disbanded and Nicholson chased mutineers over the rugged terrain of the North West Frontier. No prisoners were taken; they were either shot or hung. Nicholson had no patience with the procedure of court martial and his mark in every town was a pair of gallows, each adorned with six hanging mutineers. When Sir John Lawrence in a dispatch, asked him for details of the court martials held and a list of punishments inflicted on the rebels, Nicholson merely returned the dispatch having written on the back, 'The punishment for mutiny is death.'

He thus carried out his duties as deputy commissioner with the whip and the sword. Michael Edwards writes that 'Nicholson was a complex and tortured personality ... He was a homosexual, a repressed homosexual, disgusted by his own inclinations and one who translated his disgust into a violence manic in its manifestations.' He often personally cut off the heads of criminals and displayed them on his desk as a reminder. He felt that the idea of simply hanging rebels was maddening and he made several suggestions in writing for obscene punishments like 'flaying alive and impalement,' among others.

Nicholson loathed India and Indians. He is quoted as saying in a letter, 'I hate India and its inhabitants more every day.' He, however, wished to stay on in the country due to his messianic streak and felt he had a mission here, 'which was to spread a Christian Empire of the British in this heathen wilderness'. In an earlier war, his brother's dead body was found with his genitalia cut off and stuffed in his mouth. This further intensified his hatred and made him near psychopathic.

To create horror in the minds of rebels, Nicholson resorted to the punishment of blowing them off from cannons on parade grounds. By early June, forty of them had perished thus. It was such a gruesome practice that it had not been used for fifty years, though earlier the Mughals had on rare occasions resorted to it. The victim was lashed to cannon, the small of his back or the pit of his stomach against the muzzle, and then 'he was smeared with the blood of the Englishmen murdered by the rebels'. When the gun was fired, the head of the victim, hardly disfigured, would fly through the smoke and fall to the ground slightly blackened, followed by the arms and legs, which would also be only partially mutilated. The trunk would of course be shattered, giving off a beastly smell of burning flesh. Pieces of bone, intestines and blood would fall on the gunners and the eager spectators who had ventured too close. The vultures flying above would, with amazing skill, snap up the bits of flesh in their beaks.

All over the country, the British had proved that they were second to none when it came to brutality and their viciousness was unparalleled in history and not far removed from the later Nazi horrors in Europe.

Meanwhile, in their effort to recapture Delhi from the rebels, the British had not made much progress. They were restricted to the Ridge, which is several kilometres from the city, and desperately needed reinforcements. From Peshawar, the man selected to lead the 'military column' to Delhi was Nicholson and he was given the rank of a brigadier. This column consisted of Sikh and Punjabi Muslim sipahis. Nicholson was followed by a siege train of heavy guns, ammunition and other equipment. He arrived in Delhi in early August after a series of forced marches. Later in the month, Nicholson sallied out of the Ridge and defeated a small rebel force near Najafgarh. By mid-September, the British had received adequate reinforcements and were strong enough to make the final assault on the capital. Within the first few hours of the attack, Nicholson, the 'Hero of Delhi', who had seen hardly any action, was shot in a narrow street near Kashmiri Gate. He lingered on in great pain for nine days before he died. He was buried beneath a marble slab stolen from a pavilion in one of Bahadur Shah's gardens.

William Hodson

The son of a clergyman, William Hodson had a good education. He was at school at Rugby, followed by Trinity College at Cambridge. But he was less interested in books and more in his vocation as a 'Christian Soldier'. But there was an unfortunate flaw in the man; he was not only ruthless, but also corrupt.

Soon after he came to India, he fought in the Sikh wars. Later, he became the district commissioner at Amritsar, from where he moved on to the North West Frontier to take up the position as deputy commissioner of the Yusufzai tribal areas and adjutant of the new Corps of guides. Suddenly, however, Hodson found himself disgraced. In 1854, he was relieved of his command for falsification of regimental accounts and embezzling funds. He had also falsely accused and illegally imprisoned tribal leaders. Soon after, he killed a subedar for being involved in mutiny, but it is more likely, because Hodosn, owed the man money, which he had no intention of returning. William Dalrymple quotes a writer saying that Hodson 'was too unscrupulous to be a good soldier and was really fit only to lead Italian banditti'.

While he was pressing for an enquiry to exonerate him, the rebellion broke out and this made all the difference to him. His energy and his ruthlessness had come to the attention of the commissioner-in-chief and he was permitted to raise a new regiment of irregular cavalry, comprising mainly of Sikhs. This was called Hodson's Horse. Hodosn was also given the task to gather intelligence in and around Delhi.

In his operations, Hodson, like Nicholson, seldom bothered with legal niceties. Charles Allan quotes him as saying, 'I never like my men take prisoners, but shoot them all at once.' What is worse is that he took a sadistic pleasure in the killing.

Hodson became an efficient intelligence chief. With the help of a one-eyed 'maulvi', Rajab Ali, he set up an extensive network of spies in Delhi and even enlisted informants in the rebel army, who fed vital information to the enemy, including rebel positions, gun emplacements, and the weak spots in fortifications. The rebels had no such reliable information about the British and this must have influenced the final outcome at Delhi.

As enemy troops advanced into the capital, the rebels fought fiercely. They fought for every street and every house, and even on the first day, a third of the British force had been killed in the fighting. Hodson was, to quote him, 'horrified by the speed with which both the discipline and the morale of the army seemed to collapse'. But they regrouped and, inch by inch, the enemy advanced and, after six days of intense fighting, the hated British flag was hoisted at the Red Fort.

Then started the killing and the looting. In comparison Nadir Shah's massacre paled into insignificance. When he raised the sword arm, the massacre started, but a few lours later, he lowered his arm and it stopped. The British killing and plundering went on day after day making Delhi one big mass grave.

Hodson was an expert looter. His driving force was the desire to loot and he went about making his fortune. The historian Holmes calls Hodson 'the most notorious looter in the whole army'.

Meanwhile, Bahadur Shah Zafar and Zeenat Mahal had escaped to Humanyun's tomb. The British wanted Bahadur Shah and his family captured. The man given this job was Hodson. Through his spy network he had already been in touch with Zeenat Mahal. At the tomb, maulvi Rajab Ali, Hodson's henchman, went in and negotiated with the emperor, while Hodson and his escort hid in the ruins. The emperor's life and dignity was guaranteed and other terms settled, after which he and his queen surrendered. The road back to the capital was lined by thousands, and some walked behind the royal couple. It was a sad and cruel journey. The emperor came back a prisoner.

The next day, Hodson persuaded the general to let him go again to Humanyun's tomb in order to capture the three princes, Mirza Mughal, Khizr Sultan, and Abu Baker. Hodson rode out with an escort of 100 sowars and again sent in the negotiator Rajab Ali. The princes were given no guarantee, but seeing that the emperor had been spared, they assumed that they also would escape death. They were at the Khuni Darwaza near the city walls of Delhi, where according to Hodson's version, a large threatening crowd seemed to be preparing to rescue the princes. Another officer, however, states that it was only a small number of people and there was no threat. This latter version is also confirmed in a later account by Hodson's own orderly. Hodson's next action was horrific. He stopped the cart in which the princes were travelling and ordered them to get out and strip naked. He then shot them dead in cold blood. The brazen plunderer that he was, he then stripped the corpses of their rings and their bejeweled swords. The next day, he wrote to his sister saying, 'In 24 hours, I disposed off the principal members of the family of Timur the Tartar. I must confess I did enjoy the opportunity of ridding the earth of these wretches.' The corpses were put on public display and Hodson was warmly congratulated by all Europeans who also added, 'Hope you bag many more.' No enquiry was ordered into Hodson's heinous action.

Soon after, in March 1858, Hodson was shot dead when he was entering a palace in Lucknow looking for loot.

The regiment of irregular cavalry raised by Hodson did well during his life time, but later it was accused of cowardly behaviour, on more than one occasion, during the campaign for the pacification of Oude (Awadh). Inexplicably, and rather foolishly, a regiment Hodson's Horse, still exists in the Indian Army.

James Neill

James Neill was a particularly vicious man who justified his brutality as 'holy work, God's work'. He was a Scotsman aged forty-seven, with long military service behind him. He was proud of his faith and also of his physical prowess. Neill was a colonel in the 1st Madras fusciliers and was summoned with his men from the peace and quiet of Madras to the turbulent north. He arrived in Calcutta in May 1857 and was ordered to proceed to the relief of General Wheeler at Kanpur. While the *firanghee* soldiers found it much too grueling to march in the heat of summer, and getting his men to Banaras meant a rail journey of about 100 miles where the railway line ended, then further by horse carriages, bullock carts and the steamer on the river. Neill arrived in Banaras on 3 June, but could not go on to Allahabad and Kanpur as he was stopped by the station commander, as the situation in Banaras was dangerous and mutiny could break out at any moment. Neill insisted on disarming the local Indian troops but handled the whole process very inefficiently. The sipahis were ordered to lay down their arms, which they started doing peacefully, when suddenly European soldiers arrived on the parade ground. The sipahis assumed that like so many of their comrades elsewhere, they would be attacked after they were disarmed. The commander failed to reassure them and some sipahis reached for their arms, at which point the Europeans opened fire. The artillery was also turned on the Indian troops and there was much bloodshed.

Although the districts surrounding Banaras had been quiet, Neill encouraged the local British civilians to go out and kill anyone even suspected of being a rebel. These executions were known as 'Colonel Neill's hangings'. To quote Kaye in the 'Sepoy War', 'Volunteer hanging parties went out into the districts, and amateur exectuioners were not wanting for the occasion. One gentleman boasted of the numbers he had finished off quite "in an artistic manner", with mango trees for gibbets and elephants for drops, the victims of this wild justice being strong up, as though, for pastime, in "the form of a figure of eight".'

By the time Neill reached Allahabad, his reputation as a killer had preceded him and the Allahabad sipahis, who had so for remained loyal, now feared the worst and thus revolted as well. This time, the British were not unprepared and they managed to get the situation under control. Despite this, however, Neill decided to teach the 'niggers' a lesson and instill fear in the town. Allahabad was then bombarded and set on fire. As the people ran out of the town, they were mowed down by grapeshot. The surrounding countryside next received the weight of Neill's attention. Villages were set on fire and troops that encircled them then saw to it that the fleeing inhabitants were either burnt alive or shot dead. The historian Holmes writes in *Mutiny*, 'Old men who had done us no harm, helpless women with sucking infants at their breasts, felt the weight of our vengeance.'

Bholanath Chander in the *Travels of a Hindu,* writes that 'thousands perished and their corpses hanging from branch and signposts all over town .... For three months did eight carts daily go their rounds from sunrise to sunset to take down the corpses which hung at the crossroads and market places poisoning the air of the city and to throw their loathsome burden into the Ganges.'

Neill, who was proud of his physique, was now tortured by fatigue and sickness, and this probably redoubled his bloodthirstiness as he pursued 'God's work'. But unfortunately, all that Neill's work led to was retaliation by the rebels and the subsequent massacre of his countrymen and women at Kanpur.

The British authorities in appreciation of Neill's activities promoted him to the rank of brigadier general.

He was delayed in his onward march from Allahabad to Kanpur because of the difficulty in obtaining supplies and transport for his troops. The people in the towns and the countryside had been so terrorized by the British that no one would come forward and offer them the much needed rations or transport. Thus, by the time Neill got to Kanpur the events described in the chapter on Nana Saheb, had already taken place. General Wheeler had surrendered and he and the other British survivors of the entrenchment had been killed on the riverside. The hideous massacre at Bibighar had also taken place. Neill's actions at Banaras and Allahabad preceded the killings at Kanpur and to see Kanpur as having provoked Neill's brutalities is to forget chronology. It is more than possible that it was Neill's horrific killings of innocent people that provoked Nana Saheb.

Neill, now in charge at Kanpur, set about avenging the killings by the rebels. He wrote in a letter: 'I will show to the natives of India that the punishment inflicted by us for such deeds will be the heaviest and the most revolting to their feelings and what they must ever remember.'

On 25 July, he issued an order according to which all miscreants who took an active part in the mutiny, would be taken to Bibighar where the massacre of women and children took place and, as quoted by Michael Edwards in *Red Day*, 'they were made to crouch down, and with their mouths clean a square foot of the blood soaked floor .... The dried blood on the floor was first moistened with water and the lash of the warder was applied till the wretches kneeled down and cleaned the square foot of flooring.' After this process had been completed, the culprits were hanged. To complete the humiliation and cause most revulsion, the Hindus were buried and the Muslims, cremated.

In this context, Neill recorded in a letter, 'No doubt it is a strange law, but it suits the occasion well ...' Even here, Neill brings in God when he further states, 'I will hold my own, with the blessing and help of God. I cannot help seeing his finger in all this.'

In mid-September 1857, Neill finally arrived in Lucknow. As he was leading a column to the Residency, he was ambushed and shot through the head. So died the 'Idol of the British Army'. The grateful Queen of England awarded Neill a posthumous knighthood.

KUNWAR SINGH

Kunwar Singh (Or Kuer Singh) was a charismatic and awe-inspiring figure. He had won more victories against the British than any other leader of the 1857-59 rebellion. His battle plans were brilliant and he resorted to tactics that enabled him to inflict the most humiliating defeats. Strangely, in most books on the rebellion he has received scant attention. His exploits are either stated in a few paragraphs, or at best, covered in a short chapter. On the other hand, like the Rani of Jhansi, Kunwar Singh is remembered to this day, in the local folklore and ballads in the countryside of Shahabad in Bihar. According to the local legend, Kunwar Singh lives on and will come back to fight another day. The Indian Army has certainly not forgotten him and his pictures adorn the mess of every battalion of the Bihar regiment.

Kunwar Singh was a Rajput chief and the talukdar of Jagdishpur, which is about 80 kilometres west of Patna and close to the town of Arrah. He was from the Parmar clan and his family originally came from the holy city of Ujjain in central India. In the fourteenth century, the Parmars had expanded eastwards and after they occupied territory in Bihar, they came to be known as Ujjainia Rajputs. One branch of the family became rulers of the Dumraon state (Tawirikh-i-Ujjainia), which lies in this region. Jagdishpur was Kunwar Singh's family seat and, during its long history, it was fought over and changed hands several times. But it was the revolt of 1857 that gained Jagdishpur a place in history.

Bihar had a disturbed period in the early eighteenth century due to frequent Maratha raids. After the battles of Plassey in 1757 and that of Buxar in 1764, the British had gained control over Bihar.

Kunwar Singh's father, Sahebzada Singh, was a powerful chieftain and an interesting character. On a visit to Patna to meet the British commissioner, Sahebzada Singh got involved in a brawl and as British records of 1794 state, 'in unbounded rage and passion he drew his sword and attempted the lives of several people'. He was promptly arrested, but was released on bail. Soon after, a tiger entered the outskirts of the city and started creating pandemonium. Sahebzada Singh trailed the animal and showed considerable valour in killing the beast. In recognition of this gallant act, the case against him was dropped by the authorities. The history of the Dumraon state contains many anecdotes of his physical strength and impulsive actions. But apart from being a colourful man, Sahebzada Singh, like most of the aristocracy of those times, was extremely extravagant and ran up huge debts. When he died in 1826, he left his son and successor Kunwar Singh entangled in debts and unending litigation.

Like his father, Kunwar Singh too was spirited and adventurous. His education was rudimentary, as was usual among people of his class. When his father was alive, he lived away from Jagdishpur and built himself a large colonial bungalow with a thatched roof in the nearby jungles. Here he spent his time hunting and riding with his *sowars*.

Kunwar Singh was eighty years old at the time of the revolt, a fact confirmed by several sources. Considering the battles he fought, the life he led of a hunted guerilla leader and the hundreds of miles he traversed in the course of the rebellion, he must, despite his age have been a remarkably strong man. A British judicial officer's description of him has been quoted by General S.K. Sinha, 'Kuer Singh was a tall man about seven feet in height with long arms extending down to his knees. He had a big face with broad jaws and high cheek bones, an aquiline nose and broad high forehead, as the best Ujjainis have. He was a first-rate horseman, spearman and swordsman, also an accurate hand at the gun. All these weapons he usually manufactured at his own village of Jagdishpur, where he also manufactured gunpowder.'

Another contemporary British writer, Hale, said that 'He was a fine, noble looking old man ... his manners were at once dignified and courteous and bore the stamp of real nobility ... He had been a great sportsman and much liked by the Europeans generally.'

After his father's death in 1826 Kunwar Singh became the talukdar of Jagdishpur. His brothers also inherited some villages as part of their patrimony. But there was the inevitable dispute about the allocation among the brothers, leading to some bad blood and expensive litigation. This was all sorted out in favour of Kunwar Singh, and good relations were restored among them. The youngest brother, Amar Singh, was especially close to Kunwar Singh and fought shoulder to shoulder with him when Kunwar Singh rose against the British in 1857. Like Kunwar Singh, he was a man of strong physique and fair complexion. At the time of the uprising, he was about forty-five years old. We will talk about him later in the narrative.

Jagdishpur was a fairly large estate and, according to records, its annual revenue was Rs 3,83,000, a handsome amount for the times. After the Dumraon state, Jagdishpur was next in size in the Shahabad district. With the succession of Kunwar Singh began an era of peace and prosperity in the estate. Kunwar Singh treated his tenants most generously and in return he was loved and respected by them. When he fought the British, they rose along with him. Kunwar Singh was proud of his family seat of Jagdishpur and being aesthetically inclined he started to beautify the town. New markets were laid, wells and tanks were constructed and the civic amenities generally improved. He renovated the Jagdishpur *garh* (fort) and the imposing gate was embellished. His palace received much attention and was adorned it with weapons and firearms. He also constructed an elaborate temple for the people. It is sad to think that much of this was destroyed in the subsequent battles.

Kunwar Singh was married to a wealthy raja's daughter, but both S.K. Sinha and the historian K.K. Data mention that he also had a Muslim mistress, Dharman Bibi, and they were devoted to each other. He had a mosque constructed for her and a bazaar near Arrah that was named after her, Bibiganj. She remained with him during the days of his adversity and when, after his rebellion, he had to abandon his beloved Jagdishpur, she accompanied him into the jungles and hills in his wanderings as a guerilla fighter. But the hardships were too much for her to bear and she died during the long campaign in the arms of her heartbroken lord. Kunwar Singh had only one son, who died young, but he left Kunwar Singh with a grandson, Birbhajan Singh, on whom the old chieftain doted.

Interestingly, for most of his life, Kunwar Singh had cordial relations with the British government. He counted many of the local British officials among his friends. His hospitality was much appreciated by them and he often included them in his hunting and shooting expeditions, which were lavish affairs with elephants for shooting big game and comfortable tents for camping. William Taylor, who was the commissioner of Patna, was an especially good friend of both Kunwar Singh and his brother Amar Singh.

In 1843, there was an outbreak in the Arrah jail. The prisoners rioted and in the violence they attacked the English medical officer, who was visiting the jail. William Taylor was unable to cope with the situation and asked for Kunwar Singh's help, who promptly came and calmed down and controlled the prisoners. Taylor later wrote, 'Meanwhile I had sent for the renowned Koer Singh, the powerful landowner, who was afterwards driven into rebellion by the short sightedness of the Bengal government. He came readily and with him I entered the jail.'

Although Kunwar Singh had large landed estates, that gave him a handsome rental income, he ran into huge financial problems. He had, as mentioned earlier, inherited debts from his father. He had also spent considerable sums on the renovation of Jagdishpur. He was over-generous to his tenants and had made extensive grants for charitable purposes. The *sanad*s (Deed of Grants) relating to these are still available among the records of Shahabad Collectorate. Finally, his personal lifestyle, including his hunting expeditions, required extravagant expenditure. All these led to huge borrowings. These debts could have been cleared through sound financial management, but like most of the Rajput nobility Kunwar Singh had not been educated and had to leave his financial affairs in the hands of unscrupulous employees, who swindled him and proved to be parasites fattening on his blood. His affairs got so complicated that he and some creditors petitioned the government to take up the management of his properties, so that the debts could be liquidated from the proceeds of his estates. This arrangement did not go through and there was the danger of Kunwar Singh losing his pledged estates. The Board of Revenue also stepped in and in 1857 Kunwar Singh found himself on the brink of bankruptcy. He was deeply attached to his ancestral land and would have done anything to retain possession of it. It has been argued that joining the revolt was one last desperate step he took to save his estates. A British official named Wake had written in July 1857 to the government that 'Kunwar Singh is nominally the owner of vast estates, whilst in reality he is a ruined man, and can hardly find money to pay the interest on his debts. As long, therefore, as law and order exist, his position cannot improve: take them away and he well knows that he would become supreme in his district.'

There are, however, conflicting views on the reasons for his joining the revolt. It has been argued that Kunwar Singh's involvement in an earlier anti-British plot in 1845-46 suggests that while he maintained friendly relations with some British officials, he was opposed to the continuance of British rule. More than a decade before the Great Revolt, there had been mounting resentment against the British and a plot was hatched. The sipahis at Danapur cantonment near Patna had been approached. Various rajas and zamindars had got together at a *mela* (fair) at Sonepur. At this conclave it was decided to get the cooperation of the sipahis and raise a force with the help of the king of Nepal and the Mughal emperor at Delhi. After this, Kunwar Singh had gone to Kathmandu to seek the help of the king of Nepal and according to historian K.K. Datta, the emperor had stated that 'he will come down and erase the name and mark of the Europeans from Hindustan.'

However, before the plot came to fruition, information regarding it was leaked to the English. Various incriminating documents were found at the house of some prominent Muslim Wahabi leaders. The British took effective steps and the plot collapsed. At this time, the British were in a difficult position engaged as they were in the Anglo-Sikh Wars in the Punjab. Patna was an important communication centre on both the land and river routes from their capital in Calcutta to the Punjab. Troops and equipment were being moved along this route. Thus, despite ample evidence of Kunwar Singh's involvement in the plot, it was decided as a matter of policy, not to proceed against him as they wanted to avoid turmoil in Bihar and they felt that 'the arrest of Baboo Koer Singh will very likely be followed by a rising of the people, who are at his back.' There was also evidence against other rajas and zamindars, but they were all treated with great leniency to avoid inflaming the local population. Kaye, the historian of the revolt, succinctly calls it, 'An incident which in quiet times, might have made itself heard all over the country, but which, lost in the din of battle in that momentous winter, gave only local sound.'

Bihar was not only important to the British as it commanded the land and river route from Calcutta to the north-west; but also because there were many European indigo planters in the province and any anarchy and disorder would lead to much commercial loss, which the British, being good shopkeepers, were always averse to.

It is worth noting that in 1857 Kunwar Singh was getting involved in a plot to usurp British rule even before the uprising took place. British historian Malleson states, 'It was suspected that Kanwar Singh had been for months carrying on an active correspondence with the disaffected regiments scattered over the lower provinces.' Another historian, C.T. Metcalf, noted that Kunwar Singh 'had been in constant correspondence with Nana Saheb and had also attempted to influence the Rajas of Bihar'.

About 10 kilometres from Patna was the cantonment of Danapur, where there were three sepoy regiments and artillery. Major General Lloyd who commanded Danapur, was an old man and had served in the army for fifty-three years. There were other smaller military stations scattered over Bihar. After the outbreak at Meerut, news came pouring in about several other regiments mutinying in Delhi and the United Provinces. General Lloyd, however, decided not to disarm the Indian troops at Danapur, as the disaffection had not spread here. However, as the revolt came to Varanasi, and closer to Bihar, many Europeans panicked and left their posts in the countryside and converged in Patna. William Taylor, the commissioner here held himself responsible for the safety of the Europeans, and as General Lloyd had not disarmed the Danapur sipahis, he summoned Captain Rattray and his Sikh battalion to Patna. They were later of great help to the British. Defiance was spreading fast in Bihar and Captain Rattray reported that as he and the Sikhs were marching through the town, they were abused by the people and 'For days afterwards the Sikhs were subjected to reviling, as having come to help the *Kaffir*s (infidels).'

Taylor also believed that the Wahabi Muslims were hatching a conspiracy against the government. He identified the three ring leaders and by a dishonourable stratagem he had them brought to his house under a false pretence and arrested them. As a result, a riot broke out at Patna, which Taylor suppressed with great ferocity. Twenty-four persons were convicted for having taken part in the rioting and they were summarily hanged.

Following Taylor's reign of terror, the Indian troops at Danapur got to know that General Lloyd had received instructions from the governor general to detain one of the British regiments at Patna which was on the way to the north-west, in case he thought it desirable to disarm the troops at Danapur. Indian soldiers had also heard that at Varanasi the sipahis had been treacherously disarmed and, during the process, many had been shot down. The Danapur troops were thus deeply disturbed and alienated.

Lloyd still hesitated about disarming the local sipahis, but he finally decided on a via media. European troops were drawn up; but Lloyd gave orders that only the percussion caps with Indian troops be taken away, this rendering their firearms harmless. At the same time, they were not subjected to any humiliation as had happened in some other stations during the disarming process. But this was a half-measure because each man inexplicably still had fifteen caps left with him. These the *sipahi*s later refused to surrender when they were ordered to do so. The British soldiers were then ordered to fire on them and the mutiny was sparked off not only at Danapur but also at Sagauli, a smaller military station.

Kunwar Singh had been closely watching these developments. Even before the Danapur mutiny, he had been approached by sipahis who had rebelled at different military stations and had come back to their homes in this district. There had been rumours that he was getting involved in the revolt, though his friend William Taylor strongly refuted them. However, he summoned Kunwar Singh to Patna, but as every zamindar in those restless days, was apprehending arrest, Kunwar Singh decided not to fall into a trap and did not go to meet Taylor.

Meanwhile, the Danapur rebel sipahis marched off towards Arrah with their weapons. Because Lloyd had seized the bulk of percussion caps they were, however, severely handicapped by a shortage of ammunition. When they reached Arrah, Kunwar Singh joined them. This made a huge difference because Kunwar Singh was the feudal chieftain and if he raised the standard of rebellion; his tenants would also rise to defend their chief. Many of them were of Rajput origin and thus he was their natural leader. This then became a general revolt rather than a mutiny. Among the main lieutenants of Kunwar Singh were his brother Amar Singh and his friend Nishan Singh, who was then in his mid-sixties. He fought alongside Kunwar Singh right through, but in the last stages of the war, was captured by the British and 'blown away from a cannon'. Many other leaders had also risen and they were all out to prove that Rajput valour was not extinct.

With Kunwar Singh at their head, the rebels plundered the treasury at Arrah and released prisoners from jails. The British civilians in the town had taken refuge at Arrah House and were defended by fifty Sikhs from Rattray's battalion. General S.K. Sinha in his book argues that Kunwar Singh made no serious attempt, attacking their poorly fortified shelter because he was against all senseless killing of Europeans and, more importantly, he wanted to conserve the limited ammunition with the sipahis. This ammunition was to be used against the impending attacks of the enemy, which Kunwar Singh knew, were bound to follow. British historians have concocted a long-winded account of the heroic defence of Arrah House, against the sipahis. As one writer says, 'the defense of Ara

House, duly embellished, became part of British imperial lore'. But no effort had been made to overrun the place for the very sensible reason that enemy troops were advancing from Danapur and Buxar and dealing with them was more important, especially in view of the fact that the ammunition with the rebels was very limited. A half-hearted attempt was probably made at Arrah House by a small group of sipahis, but it was foiled by the Sikhs in British pay.

It was obvious that General Lloyd had bungled the disarming of the sipahis. After the rebel sipahis had left Danapur and fled towards Arrah, Lloyd was finally prevailed upon to take action. On 26 July, a steamer with a detachment of riflemen was sent on the Sone river to intercept the rebels, but they had already crossed the river and liberated Arrah. A second steamer was sent to Arrah but it got stuck on the sand bank. A third steamer, which had arrived from Allahabad with passengers for Calcutta, was then requisitioned and this was sent with a force under the command of Captain Dunbar. The total strength of this force was 340 British and 70 Sikhs.

Kunwar Singh was expecting them and he had a well-laid out plan to deal with this enemy force. Dunbar arrived late in the evening and immediately started his march to Arrah. He was totally deceived by reports that had been deliberately planted, that the sipahis were in a state of panic at his advance and would not put up any effective resistance. It was a dark moonless night, but overconfident and careless, he pressed on. He was advised by his deputy to halt for the night as the troops needed rest and food, but Dunbar ignored this advice and advanced with speed towards Arrah. He had no vanguard or scouts in front and marched blindly into the trap Kunwar Singh had laid for him. Kunwar Singh's men had taken up positions in a small forest, waiting to ambush the enemy. As soon as the British troops appeared on a raised causeway, the rebels opened heavy musket fire. Dunbar was among the first to be killed. As Sinha says, 'Caught in a perfectly executed ambush, the enemy suffered heavy casualties. The British in their white uniforms could be easily picked up even in the darkness of the night. The sepoys were mostly bare bodied and their brown skin merged with the darkness of the night ... A disastrous retreat followed and the sepoys maintained pressure.

Soon all cohesion was lost … The retreat became a rout'. Isabel Giberne Sieveking in *A Turning Point in the Indian Mutiny* describes the ambush, 'from the front of our column, from the right flank, from the left flank came through the darkness with fatal effect, the heavy shower of musket balls … of the 400 men who had gone out the day before, full of health and hope, one half had been left behind to gorge the vultures and the jackals and of those who returned only about fifty were unwounded. Since then nearly 100 more from wounds and exposure have died'. The sipahis had each only a few percussion caps left, otherwise the British would have been annihilated.

On 30 July, General Lloyd reported by telegraph to the commander-in-chief, 'The result of the expedition to Arrah has been, I regret to say, very disastrous, owing entirely to the mismanagement of the officer in command, the late Capt. Dunbar.' A few weeks later, he again informed the commander-in-chief, 'Koer Singh is said to have mustered strongly on his own account; sometimes said to meditate an attack on Patna … All the boats on the river Sone are in his possession.'

The shock of this disaster completely unnerved the enemy. William Taylor ordered all district officers to come to Patna. This was not approved by the higher authorities and later Taylor was removed from the commissionership of Patna and posted to a distant district in East Bengal, where he resigned in disgust. The Governor General Lord Canning's correspondence over the incident shows great despondency.

However, there was much rejoicing at Arrah at this victory. Kunwar Singh was felicitated and hailed as the maharaja. The district of Shahabad had been liberated and British control ended. Kunwar Singh then set up his own administration with police arrangements, etc. But the Rajput knew that all this was short-lived and the British, who in fact expected him to plan an attack on Patna, were bound to retaliate.

Major Vincent Eyre had distinguished himself in the Afghan War and was later posted with the Gwalior contingent. He was an old man, but on learning of the British rout at Arrah, he advanced with a column from Buxar. In addition to the Highlanders, he was joined by Captain L'Estrange and his party of fusiliers. Kunwar Singh realized that he may not be able to ambush Eyre as the latter had been forewarned by the fate of Dunbar. He made plans for this and destroyed a few bridges on Eyre's route, but many vital ones were left standing. Kunwar Singh had a force that was numerically superior, but his men suffered from a shortage of ammunition. Eyre's soldiers were also equipped with Enfield rifles and importantly, artillery. Against this, Kunwar Singh's sipahis with their old muskets were no match as their range was much shorter than the enemy's rifles. They also did not have a single piece of artillery. Like Dunbar, Eyre was also waylaid by the sipahis, but with superior firepower, broke through. Eyre also took the precaution of never marching in the dark of night.

As Eyre advanced towards Bibiganj, the sipahis harassed his column along the way and kept on a running battle, but the range of the Enfield rifles kept Kunwar Singh's forces at a distance. From accounts of the battle of Bibiganj, it would appear that it was a hard-fought one. A broken bridge near the town afforded good protection to the Indians. From behind this, their fire was effective and the British forces had to find cover behind some brick kilns. As the distance between the two structures was not much, the longer range of the English rifles did not prove an advantage. The firing went on for several hours and the fusiliers were losing ground. What seemed to have turned the tide were the three cannons with Eyre they were now used by him to fire grape shot, which caused heavy casualties among the sipahis and broke their assaults. Next, Eyre ordered a bayonet charge, against which one flank of Kunwar Singh's sipahis wilted and this forced their retreat. Eyre wrote that 'The Raja (Kunwar Singh) was present in person in this action.' A second eyewitness says about him, 'Someone of rank came on to the plain which separated us. He fired three or four times from a rifle …. But the bearing of Kunwar Singh even at that distance was striking. No indecent haste, no seeking cover, he retired as coolly as he came.' This quote clearly shows Kunwar Singh's disregard for personal danger.

The battle of Bibiganj turned the tide of the rebellion in Bihar. Arrah was once again in enemy hands. A reign of terror was let loose on the town and the gallows were kept busy at work. It was a deliberate British policy to hold a public spectacle of horror to discourage further rebellion. Kunwar Singh never once indulged in atrocities on the Europeans. Historian S.N. Sen quotes several British writers to support this and I quote only one writer, Hall who says, 'During the time the Europeans at Arrah were shut up, Kunwar Singh had several families in his power, all of who were found uninjured at his departure, indeed we are not aware that he ever participated in the atrocities ...'.

After the battle at Bibiganj, Kunwar Singh retired to his ancestral castle at Jagdishpur with some sipahis. Meanwhile, Eyre got further reinforcements of British and Sikh soldiers and followed him to Jagdishpur. Kunwar Singh offered stiff resistance to Eyre, but muskets had no chance against howitzers. The new temple and other civic works that Kunwar Singh had erected at Jagdishpur at great expense were demolished. Kunwar Singh's palace and fort were reduced to rubble. Apart from this shameless destruction, the British indulged in their usual barbaric public hangings of all suspected rebels. They also confiscated Kunwar Singh's estate and announced a reward of Rs 10,000 for anyone providing information leading to his arrest. Exulting over this victory, Eyre wrote from Jagdishpur, 'I am destroying the town and preparing to blow up the palace and principal buildings around it ... set fire to the residences of the two brothers of Koer Singh.'

For the various actions around Arrah, including the disastrous retreat of Dunbar's column, the British awarded three Victoria Crosses. Eyre was also recommended for the award but the recommendation was not accepted. General Lloyd, who had mismanaged the disarming of the sipahis, escaped a court martial but his military career was ignominiously terminated.

Kunwar Singh's army had suffered one defeat and his ancestral stronghold, which he loved, had been destroyed, but the old lion still had his fangs bared and was willing to fight. There were yet battles to be won. To put heart back into the men from his estate, he said, 'Wherever I am, that is Jagdishpur.'

He still had about 1,000 sipahis with him but, unable to find shelter in the jungles of his estate, he moved with them to the hills of Rohtas. It was reported to the enemy that he had in addition 'four elephants, fourteen camels, a lot of horses but no ammunition'. The last was his main problem. His brother Amar Singh meanwhile continued to harass the enemy from a nearby hilly retreat.

The presence of the brothers in the area threatened the Grand Trunk Road, the main British communication. But Kunwar Singh had a grander vision. He believed that the war against the enemy would be won or lost not in Bihar, but in the main theatre, which was north India. He therefore decided to establish contact with the other great leaders including Nana Saheb and Tatya Tope.

With this in view, Kunwar Singh marched from the vicinity of Mirzapur to Rewa, as the raja was a distant kinsman. But the latter remained loyal to the British. As Kunwar Singh advanced towards the town, the raja and his family fled. Kunwar Singh was, opposed by Colonel Hinde who commanded the Rewa army. There was a skirmish; but Kunwar Singh felt that this distraction was pointless and he decided to proceed with his men to the nearby state of Banda. The Nawab of Banda (a descendent of Peshwa Baji Rao and his Muslim mistress Mastani) welcomed Kunwar Singh into his capital.

By this time Delhi had fallen to the British and Kunwar Singh had to adjust his plan according to the changed circumstances. From Banda he went to Kalpi at the invitation of Nana Saheb and the Gwalior contingent to participate in the projected assault on Kanpur. Kunwar Singh had arrived in Kalpi at the end of October 1857, after a journey covering over 400 miles, fighting in several skirmishes, evading pursuit by the British, camping at different locations, crossing numerous monsoon-flooded rivers, riding or sometimes being carried in a palanquin through thick jungles. He was eighty years old and it would have been a tough journey even for a man half his age. S.K. Sinha states that he also suffered two personal tragedies during this long march. His mistress Dharman Bibi, who had accompanied him, could not stand the rigours of the journey and succumbed to illness on the way. Kunwar Singh had lost his only son several years earlier, but now his grandson Birbhajan Singh, on whom Kunwar Singh doted, also died, extinguishing the line of his direct descendents. However, none of this daunted him and his determination to fight on did not waver.

Kanpur was an important centre of the revolt. When the commander-in-chief, Sir Colin Campbell, marched from here to relieve the British garrison besieged at the residency in Lucknow, he left General Windham to defend Kanpur. Tatya Tope was in command of the rebels consisting of the Gwalior contingent and the sipahis of Kunwar Singh and the Nawab of Banda plus other rebel sipahis from Kalpi. Tatya Tope attacked the city from one direction, while Nana Saheb advanced from another direction. Kunwar Singh took a leading part in this operation and General Windham's forces were soundly beaten. The enemy was forced to leave the city and retreat to its entrenchment. The British suffered heavy casualties and lost a considerable part of their stores. However, the commander-in-chief, who was located in Lucknow, rushed back when he heard of the disaster at Kanpur. Most unfortunately, Tatya Tope had not destroyed the bridge across the Ganga, between Kanpur and Lucknow. The enemy forces were at their last gasp at Kanpur, but help had now arrived and Tatya lost the chance of his life.

After the defeat at Kanpur, Tatya Tope asked Kunwar Singh to join him at Kalpi. But as General S.K. Sinha says in his book, Kunwar Singh had realized that in the three conventional battles that he had fought at Bibiganj, Jagdishpur and Kanpur, the Indians had suffered defeats. However, he had succeeded admirably in guerilla operations against Dunbar at Arrah, or on raids on the British lines of communication in Bihar. The enemy had superior firepower in their Enfield rifles and their artillery and also had superior discipline. Thus, Kunwar Singh felt that it would not be wise to engage the British in set piece battles. He preferred guerilla warfare. He seemed to be following the recommendation of another rebel, Khan Bahadur Khan, who had said:

> Do not attempt to meet the regular columns of the infidels because they are superior to you in discipline and organisation and have big guns. But watch their movements, guard all *ghat*s on the rivers, intercept their communications; stop their supplies, cut up their *dak*s and posts; keep constantly hanging about their camps; give them no rest. (Quoted by the contemporary journalist W.H. Russell)

Keeping this in mind, Kunwar Singh did not join the Maratha chiefs at Kalpi but instead went to the most important seat of the war, Lucknow. This was in December 1857 and the British had been under siege at the Residency in Lucknow for seven or eight months, while the town was in the hand of rebels.

Begum Nusrat Mahal of Awadh and the young Nawab were still the rulers and they welcomed Kunwar Singh at their court. He was invested with robes of honour and was further granted a *firman* for Azamgarh. In February 1858, Kunwar Singh was a gain on the move with his rebel sipahis and other followers towards Azamgarh.

Meanwhile, the British had not only regained Delhi and Kanpur, but were also, planning the final attack on Lucknow. By moving soldiers from Delhi and Punjab, they had greatly increased their strength in the Awadh area. The king of Nepal had also sent a large contingent of Gurkhas towards Lucknow. In all these moves, the Azamgarh area had been denuded of British defenders. The old Rajput sized up the situation immediately and advanced towards Atrauli, a village 30 kilometres from Azamgarh. The Raja of Nurhurpur and Raja Maan Singh, who had also risen against the British, joined Kunwar Singh, as well as a considerable body of sipahis with four or five cannons. This was now late March 1858.

Colonel Milman who commanded the station, marched against him, but the wily Kunwar Singh outmaneuvered him completely. He gave Milman the impression that he was ready to give battle, but as the British forces advanced and shots were exchanged, Kunwar Singh's men retreated. Milman thought that they had lost their nerve and the battle had been won. The British relaxed, disarmed, stacked their weapons and got busy with breakfast. As soon as Kunwar Singh received intimation of this, he attacked with full force. There was outright consternation and panic among the enemies and they retreated pell-mell, abandoning their equipment and not stopping till they got to Azamgarh. From there, Milman sent frantic messages for help. But Kunwar Singh advanced further and captured Azamgarh. Colonel Dames, who was in Ghazipur hurried to rescue, with forces that included artillery. He was also beaten back and took shelter in the entrenchment. Azamgarh was now firmly under Kunwar Singh's control.

The fear among the British now was that Kunwar Singh may attack Arrah or even Varanasi. The commissioner of Patna, in a long report to the government at Calcutta, wrote in mid-April 1858, 'Colonel Milman has abandoned his tents and baggage at Atrauli and has shut himself up in an entrenchment ... If Kuer Singh (Kunwar Singh) lands in Arrah there cannot be a doubt that the hopes of all the disaffected in the surrounding districts will be raised ... It must be realised that his name is a watchword throughout Bihar, that he is looked up to by the Rajputs of Bihar as the chief par excellence.'

Kunwar Singh may well have made the attempt to attack Varanasi next, but by now the British had re-established control over most of north India. Lucknow had been recaptured and their military resources had been hugely augmented. The Governor General Lord Canning had shifted from Calcutta to Allahabad to be closer to the action. Deeply troubled by the two successive defeats of British troops by Kunwar Singh, he deputed Lord Mark Kerr to advance from Allahabad with the 13 Light Cavalry. As he neared Azamgarh, Kunwar Singh tried to ambush his forces. However, Kerr broke through, though he suffered heavy casualties. He did not take further action but awaited reinforcements. A second strong force under Sir Edward Luggard was then sent from Lucknow, which not only included several British regiments, but also a strong contingent of Sikhs. The whole force was supported by heavy artillery. Kunwar Singh knew he had no chance against such a formidable opposition and decided to withdraw to his home province, Bihar. He, however, left about 2,000 men to harass the enemy, employing guerilla tactics.

Meanwhile, as part of his withdrawal, Kunwar Singh fought a series of brilliant rearguard actions in order to wear out the enemy. It is said that 'Withdrawal is the most difficult operation of war.' One such action of Kunwar Singh is described by Malleson: 'He kept General Douglas at bay till he had secured two lines of retreat for his main columns, which he had divided. He then fell back leisurely and though many of his men were cut up, they maintained to the end of the day their determined attitude. As soon as Douglas's pursuit relaxed, the two columns reunited and took up positions for the night.' Sir Edward Luggard states that he had given orders 'to pursue and use utmost endeavours to capture Kunwar Singh … But they failed owing to the regularity and devoted courage with which the retreat was covered'. He goes on to refer to Kunwar Singh as 'a born strategist'. In this manner Kunwar Singh's troops withdrew till they reached the river Ganga.

The British had given orders that all boats on the banks be removed to prevent Kunwar Singh's troops from crossing and threatened severe punishment against those who did not obey. They also had British gunboats on the Ganga at the *ghat*s where they thought he would affect a passage. With the people's sympathy being with the rebels, however, Kunwar Singh could find boats where he wanted them and where he was short of boats, he used elephants to cross the Ganga. By the time Douglas's forces reached, Kunwar Singh's men were safely across and the enemy gunboats were nowhere in sight.

In battle, Kunwar Singh was usually where it raged most furiously, so that his men could emulate him. While crossing the river, he saw to it that his comrades had crossed safely before he boarded one of the last boats. But as his boat was in mid-river a cannon ball fired from the bank shattered his left arm. The only way to treat a wound in those days to prevent a deadly infection was amputation. Kunwar Singh took a sharp sword and with one stroke, this old man severed the injured limb and threw it into the sacred stream as his last offering. The British forces that had arrived by now were too exhausted to make the effort to pursue the old warrior further.

Kunwar Singh was now on his way to his beloved but devastated home Jagdishpur. The people were overjoyed to see their hero again. His brother, Amar Singh, who had continued to fight the British in this region, now rushed back from the Kaimur hills to join him. The flag of Jagdishpur was once more raised on his palace. But the old lion had returned to his lair only to die. However, he was not dead yet and had still a battle to fight and a victory to win. Sipahis from the neighbouring area rallied to Kunwar Singh's standard and he immediately started preparing for an enemy attack. Each day added to his strength as more and more sipahis arrived.

Le Grand, who had been with Eyre when they had earlier fought jointly against Kunwar Singh, was now in command at Arrah and Bibiganj. He set out for Jagdishpur with his British soldiers and Sikhs along with supporting cannons. But Le Grand, like Dunbar, had underestimated Kunwar Singh and had not taken adequate precautions in his advance. Thick jungles surrounded this area and as soon as the enemy forces entered these jungles, Kunwar Singh ambushed them. The fire from his sipahis from all directions was so strong that there was total panic and confusion. Le Grand was forced to order a retreat and this soon degenerated into panic-stricken flight. Kunwar Singh's horses pursued them, cutting down the enemy mercilessly. Le Grand was killed and British casualties were heavy, with two-thirds killed or wounded. Their cannons were also captured. It is recorded that it was only the Sikhs who showed some courage in this retreat, while the others forgot all discipline and threw order to the winds.

The eighty-year-old fighter had done all that was humanly possible and his last victory was a fitting revenge. When he died a couple of days later of his wounds, Jagdishpur was still his and the golden standard flew resplendent on his castle.

Finally, it must be repeated, and it is a fact confirmed by various historians that Kunwar Singh was an embodiment of Rajput chivalry. While the British perpetrated the most hideous atrocities on the rebels, Kunwar Singh treated the enemies under his control with consideration, and released them unharmed.

In contrast, Neill's atrocities which have been mentioned elsewhere in this book, were unbelievable. Then there was another sadist Hodson, also mentioned earlier. Both these savages have been made into great heroes by British historians. However, a few months into the war, both got their just desserts when they were shot down by the sipahis.

When Kunwar Singh was busy outside Bihar, his brother Amar Singh had established himself in the Kaimur hills and began a prolonged guerilla war against the enemy forces. He had a few hundred cavalry men and six cannons, which had been manufactured in Jagdishpur. On Kunwar Singh's death, the command of his troops devolved on Amar Singh. He also had the assistance of an able compatriot, Hare Krishan Singh, who had earlier fought alongside Kunwar Singh. The historian S.N. Sen writes,

> Amar Singh was no military genius but he had inherited the courage and resolution of his Rajput ancestors. Secure in the fidelity of his tenants, which rose above the temptation of high rewards, Amar Singh ran a parallel government in the district of Shahabad. He appointed his own magistrates and judges and even had a prison. Just as the British government and set a price on his head, he also set a price on the heads of British officials.

Thus, the movement in Shahabad had all the dignity of a national revolt and was supported openly by the population of the district.

The British were not sure whether Kunwar Singh was alive or dead and as they had a healthy respect for his fighting abilities, they decided to send strong forces against him. Three British armies converged in Arrah. Brig. Douglas came from Danapur, Gen. Luggard from Azamgarh and Col. Cornfield marched from Sasaram. Amar Singh was pitted against heavy odds and he realized that in an open fight he had no chance against his enemies. He, therefore, did not move out of the dense jungle refuge and adopted guerilla tactics. He would come out in quick lightining raids, cut off and loot their supplies and retire to his hideouts in the thickest part of the forest. Luggard tried to 'cut broad roads' into the forest to get at the rebels, but they used to scatter and elude his grasp. These tactics completely tired out the British troops who were also miserable due to the heat. Luggard wrote from Jagdishpur in May 1858 to the Chief of Staff, 'I fear it will be most difficult for me to expel them with the means at my disposal.' Finally, Gen. Luggard, not being able to stand the strain of this jungle warfare, relinquished his command on grounds of his failing health.

This guerilla warfare went on for several months and Amar Singh's raids became more daring. He crossed the river and raided important towns such as Arrah and Gaya. He plundered and destroyed government property, broke open jails and released prisoners. Malleson, in his history of the revolt says, 'Till the pacification at the close of the year, this contest in western Bihar assumed all the character of guerilla warfare. The rebels surrendered, they were beaten, they were pursued, only again to reappear. From April till December, they kept the district in continuous turmoil.'

Brig. Douglas was getting desperate and he tried encircling the jungle and sent in seven columns simultaneously from different directions to ferret out the rebels. The British infantry, for obvious reasons, could not move as quickly as the rebels who knew the forests intimately. Finally, Douglas was advised to use mounted infantry. These mounted columns were more successful and forced three engagements. Finally, they cornered Amar Singh and his men in a swampy village and inflicted heavy casualties. Amar Singh was forced to flee with his forces to the Kaimur hills. Near the end of 1858, Douglas again attacked him there. This time, he was successful in destroying the rebel army.

Amar Singh escaped to the Terrai in Nepal in order to join Nana Saheb. Rana Jang Bahadur of Nepal, however, pursued him and after finally, capturing him handed him over to the British. They jailed him in Gorakhpur, where he died in 1860.

RANI OF JHANSI

History is written by the victors. For the ninety years of British rule after the mutiny, Rani Lakshmi Bai was the 'Jezebel of India', the 'heathen who could forgive no injuries', the 'horrid Rani' and 'an ardent, daring, licentious woman', among a host of other epithets and descriptions. But then, for the last several decades since India's independence, the legend of Lakshmi Bai has lived on. It is the legend of a brave, courageous woman; a beautiful woman, and above all, an upright and god-fearing woman.

Strangely, there is not much literature about her and she lives more in the ballads, folktales and stories of Bundelkhand than in written accounts. She has often been compared to Joan of Arc, though the latter has inspired 12,000 volumes in French alone. It should be understood that the revolt was suppressed with great ferocity and no Indian dared at that time to write freely about the events of 1857-59. Despite this, a few eyewitness accounts in regional languages have survived.

Vishnu Godse, a learned Brahmin priest, was in Jhansi during the siege and he has written an eyewitness account of the events, *Ankhon Dekha Ghader*. It is interesting and authentic, and reflects the common man's view of the rebellion. Because of the terror unleashed by the British after the mutiny, Godse's account could not be published till fifty years after his death.

The Rani of Jhansi is probably the most remarkable woman in Indian history. She was on scene for a brief period of five years but emerged as the most outstanding and charismatic leader of the great revolt of 1857-59. Even her enemies rated her as 'the best and bravest of the rebel leaders'. In her short but luminous career, she did more than many rulers could aspire to do in several lifetimes. She fought British injustice in the great halls and offices of Calcutta and London and when that was not adequate, she fought their tyranny and greed in the thick of battle. She ruled Jhansi for the benefit of her people, always putting them above everything else. She gave them comfort and prosperity and won not just their loyalty but their hearts. The Rani made heroes out of the common people of Jhansi.

The kingdom over which the Rani ruled included the capital city of Jhansi and several other towns and villages in the surrounding districts. The fort of Jhansi is built on a steep rock on one side of the city and commands the whole countryside. A wide expanse of open ground separates the fort from the city. This fort was one of the major Maratha strongholds in central India under the Peshwas.

Jhansi was medium sized when compared to other Indian states. In the early 1850s, it is estimated to have covered an area of approximately 5,000 square kilometres. The state was part of an area known as Bundelkhand. The countryside was dotted with fortresses, many of them centuries old. Jhansi was part of the Maratha Confederacy, which was headed by the Peshwa and included the powerful kingdoms of Scindia of Gwalior, Holkar of Indore and Gaekwar of Baroda. In 1804, the ruler of Jhansi seeing the ascendant star of the British detached Jhansi from the crumbling Maratha Confederacy and signed a treaty with the British in which a crucial clause was that 'the British guaranteed the state to the ruler and his heirs in perpetuity'.

The Rani's ancestors were Karhada Brahmins but they forsook their traditional role as priests and scholars and chose to be soldiers and administrators. They came from the small town of Wai near Satara in Maharashtra. This area with its numerous mountains and fortresses was the heartland of Shivaji's power. Lakshmi Bai, brought up as she was at the ex-Peshwa's court, was inspired by tales of Maratha valour and she hero-worshipped Shivaji as a child. Lakshmi Bai's father, Moropant Tambe, became a close confidant and advisor to the Peshwa's brother Chimaji Appa.

Peshwa Baji Rao-II was defeated by the British in 1818. He had to leave Pune and live in exile at Bithur, a small town near Kanpur. His brother, Chimaji Appa, was also exiled but chose to live in Varanasi. Lakshmi Bai's father, Moropant Tambe, went with Chimaji to Varanasi, on a modest salary of fifty rupees a month.

Chimaji Appa lived in royal style and built himself a palace on the banks of the Ganges. Moropant and his wife Bhagirathi lived in a wing of this palace. They had a happy married life and one child, a daughter whom they called Manakarnika. This is one of the names given to the holy river Ganga, in whose lap she was born. We do not know the exact date of Manakarnika's birth, but according to British writers, she must have been born in 1827 or 1828. Manakarnika was called Manu till the time of her marriage. Lakshmi Bai was the name given to her by her husband's family and it was how she was known after she became the maharani.

Moropant's wife, Bhagirathi, was remarkably beautiful and she passed on her good looks to her daughter. She was also a religious woman and spent much of her time in reading the Hindu epics, performing puja and observing the many stipulated fasts. Bhagirathi died when her daughter was only four or five years old but she still managed to instill in her daughter a sense of piety and an uprightness, which always remained with Lakshmi Bai.

Manu was happy in her early childhood, playing on the banks of the Ganga, loved and fussed over by her doting parents. But the stories of her childhood suggest that while she was a lively and high-spirited little girl, she was also very stubborn and difficult to control.

Chimaji Appa died in 1832 and the Tambe family had to move to Bithur. Here, Moropant joined the exiled court of the ex-Peshwa. Soon after having moved to Bithur, however, Bhagirathi also died and the task of bringing up Manu fell upon her father. In 1838, Gangadhar Rao became the maharaja of Jhansi. He was to be the future husband of Rani Lakshmi Bai.

At Bithur, Manu came into contact with the Peshwa's son, Nana Saheb, as well as Nana's nephew, Rao Saheb, and Tatya Tope. These three, like herself, were destined to play major roles in the revolt of 1857. Nana, Rao and Tatya were several years older than Manu but they seem to have been very fond of her because of her high spirits and her charm. Some writers have contended that these stories of her friendship with the three are mere fiction because they were much older. That hardly seems a good enough reason. Bithur was, after all, a small town and all of them were connected with the ex-Peshwa's court, and so the families must have been close.

The old Peshwa became particularly fond of Manu and started calling her Chhabeli because she was a pretty child and full of fun. As there was no woman in Moropant's household and because he could not give adequate time to Manu, she spent much of her time with Nana, Rao and Tatya. In their company she became quite a tomboy. She followed their example and learned to ride, shoot and wield the sword. She, in fact, became an excellent rider and an expert swords woman, abilities which stood her in good stead and which she put to much practical use in the later training of her troops and in her personal encounters with the enemy. She was also keen on physical exercise and also followed wrestling matches with avid interest. She ran races, flew kites and was better than most boys in all these activities.

While all these were proper skills for boys in highborn families, they had little place in the traditional upbringing of a Brahmin's daughter. It has been suggested that her father, informed about her exceptional horoscope at birth, which foretold a royal future, had deliberately groomed her from her childhood for the role of a queen who would lead armies.

On their cross-country rides, Manu used to tag along with Nana, Rao and Tatya. The story goes that on one such occasion, as two of the boys and Manu were galloping across the country, Nana, in trying to avoid a low branch of a tree, fell off his horse. He had a big gash on his head and lost much blood. On their return, much fuss was made about Nana's injury; it was dressed and bandaged and Nana was made to rest. Manu found all this very amusing and said to him, 'Your forefathers were great warriors and look at you being coddled like this for a small cut in the head.'

Nana, peeved and nursing a headache, said, 'Manu, you are a nuisance and you talk too much. Now away with you.'

The next day, Nana chose to ride on an elephant and Manu again had a dig at him saying, 'Nana perhaps finds horse-riding a bit too tough and so has chosen an easy seat on the elephant.'

Nana, now thoroughly irritated, refused to let her accompany him on the *howda* of the elephant. This enraged Manu, who got on her horse and riding close to Nana's elephant, shouted at him, 'You wait and see! For your one elephant, I will have ten. Mark my words!'

An advantage that Manu got from her association with the three men was that she got an education. She used to sit with them for their lessons and so she learned to read and write. This was not usual for girls at that time. She was highly intelligent and, apart from Marathi and Hindi, she learned Sanskrit and picked up some Persian, which was the court language of the Mughals.

Manu became a forceful and determined person. Unlike other girls of her time, she was not shy or reticent, but ready to speak her mind. She was also, as we see later, logical and effective in debate. Thus endowed with beauty, intellect and character, she had all the makings of a charismatic leader.

Vishnu Godse has given a description of Manu in her early teens. He says she was tall and slim, with a swan-like neck. Light of complexion, she had an oval face, a fine nose and large expressive eyes, as beautiful as the lotus. She was bright and full of chatter, and people took to her immediately. She was aptly called Chhabeli.

When Manu was about twelve years old, it was time for her father to find a suitable match for her. The suitor had to be a Brahmin belonging to the Karhada sect. Suitors there were aplenty, horoscopes were compared, but no one could be identified. She was a gem of great value and a royal future had been foretold. Time passed and Moropant's friends urged him not to delay any further as the girl had reached puberty, which in those days, was considered the right age for marriage. Soon a year was gone and still there was no prospect. Moropant, worried, spent many a sleepless night. Then came a proposal from the Maharaja of Jhansi, Gangadhar Rao.

Gangadhar Rao was an able and scholarly man and did much to pull the state of Jhansi out of the morass into which his previous two predecessors had led it. His first problem was law and order which had deteriorated to dangerous proportions. The Bundela Rajput chieftains of the state had become a law unto themselves and hurled defiance from their mountain fortresses. Gangadhar dealt with this and restored order, but, unfortunately, this was with help from the British.

One of his notable achievements was that he built an excellent library of rare books from all parts of the country. The Jhansi library was famous for its collection of Sanskrit books. Unfortunately, this library was burnt down after Jhansi fell to the British. Gangadhar was aesthetically inclined and did much to architecturally improve the town of Jhansi. Theatre was another absorbing interest and he was a patron of its actors and actresses. Jhansi became a model for good administration and efficiency. The people loved and admired him. The neighbouring Bundela rulers of Panna, Orchha, Datia and Chattarpur respected him and called him Kaka Saheb or uncle and often asked for his advice for their personal or official problems.

After Gangadhar lost his first wife, he did not marry for several years, even though the couple had remained childless. However, in 1842, Gangadhar decided that it was time to look for a suitable bride. Not having an heir was a constant source of worry not only for him, but also for the people of Jhansi, as this gave the British a chance to interfere in the succession.

The ex-Peshwa at Bithur was consulted for a suitable girl and he promptly suggested Manu. Gangadhar's emissary was very impressed by the lovely young girl, bright of eye and lithe of limb. Gangadhar readily agreed and when word reached Bithur, there was much celebration. Manu was going to be a maharani. But Manu had not even set eyes on Gangadhar. She was to be a maharani, but what was the maharaja like?

A few weeks later, Moropant, Manu and a few of their relatives and friends were invited to Jhansi by Gangadhar. They stayed at a *haveli* and she had her first glimpse of him as he passed by the street on horseback. She saw a middle-aged man who was stern looking. Though he sat well with tired eyes in the saddle, he seemed a strong personality.

In May 1842, the maharaja and Manu were married at Jhansi. As was the custom, her name was changed by the family to Lakshmi Bai, after the presiding goddess. The wedding was celebrated with much splendour. Cannons boomed a salute from the ramparts of the fort and fireworks lit the sky. The couple walked round the fire seven times, and the priest tied one end of Lakshmi Bai's sari to the maharaja's sash. As he did so, Lakshmi Bai said clearly and audibly, 'Panditiji, make the knot very firm'. A bride was supposed to be modest and shy, but Lakshmi Bai was neither. All the guests were startled and gasped but Gangadhar was touched.

Time passed peacefully and happily. Moropant Tambe was made a *sardar* of the state and was granted a *jagir* (estate). Soon after, he took a second wife, Chimabai, a lady from Jhansi.

Gangadhar was an orthodox Hindu and Lakshmi Bai soon found that as a maharani, she must remain in purdah. She was only fourteen or fifteen years old and after the comparative freedom at Bithur, she found the seclusion of purdah most irksome.

The Khas Mahal (main palace) was situated inside the fort. Exquisite taste and luxury combined to make it a fitting abode for the maharani. The palace was surrounded by a garden, beyond which was a large ground that was used for parades. The parade ground was a great boon for Lakshmi Bai. Since she was not allowed outside the fort, she used it for riding, physical exercise and other activities. Lakshmi Bai also started what was later to develop into a regiment for women. She started training her companions and maid servants in horsemanship and drill, as well as other physical exercises.

Gangadhar spent much of his time at dance and theatre performances, which were his absorbing interests. One evening, he asked Lakshmi Bai if she would like to attend one of the performances. She replied, 'Maharaj, I am not interested in make belief. I am more interested in the people of Jhansi, in their welfare, in ruling the state.'

Gangadhar pondered over her answer and then asked her, 'Would you like to get acquainted with matters of government and the state?'

'There is nothing I would like more, Maharaja,' replied a delighted Lakshmi Bai.

Soon, meetings and discussions with the *diwan* (chief minister) and other senior officials in the army and administration became a feature of her life. A few months later, she gently chided Gangadhar on his spending more time at the theatre than on governing. She was particularly worried about the British presence in Jhansi. Under the treaty with them, an assistant political officer had been posted at Jhansi, as well as sipahis under British officers; Gangadhar was reconciled to the situation and saw no alternative.

As time passed, Gangadhar became fond of the unusual and striking woman who was his wife. In 1851, he took her on a pilgrimage to her birthplace, Varanasi, as well as Gaya, Prayag and other places of religious interest. The maharaja and maharani were away for six months and when they returned to Jhansi, they were given a warm welcome by the people, who turned out in thousands to see the royal procession headed by scores of elephants. Gangadhar and Lakshmi Bai sat in a gold-plated *howda* on Sidhwakas, the maharaja's favourite elephant.

One reason for the excitement was also that there were reports that Lakshmi Bai was expecting a child. It had been seven years since they had been married. And there was great rejoicing when a son was born. Gangadhar, a bit infirm by now, was especially delighted with his infant son. Lord Dalhousie, the governor general, would not be able to get his talons on Jhansi. But the rejoicing did not last long. When the heir was only three months old, he died. The couple was disconsolate, as were the people of Jhansi.

Soon after, Gangadhar's health started deteriorating. He was haunted by the prospect of his state being annexed by the British. The custom of adoption was well established and accepted. However, Gangadhar was apprehensive about Lord Dalhousie, who had taken over as governor general a few years earlier. Dalhousie's main objective seemed to be to absorb Indian states into British territory without any moral or legal justification. He had already grabbed a few states where the rulers had died without natural heirs. Gangadhar knew that should he die without an heir, the Jhansi state would lapse, but should he seek to adopt, the case might be decided by the government in his favour.

When Gangadhar finally realized that he was seriously ill and the end was near, he adopted a child from another branch of the family. The boy, Anand Rao, was five years old and was descended from Gangadhar's grandfather, which made him part of the royal family. The adoption was therefore regular and correct in the eyes of the people.

The adoption ceremonies were conducted at Gangadhar's bedside, in the presence of the nobles of the court. The maharaja had been careful enough to invite two British representatives, Major Ellis, the assistant political agent and his colleague, so that they might officially witness the adoption. The child was given a new name, Damodar Rao. Gangadhar then handed over a letter for the governor general. He requested that 'The administration of the state should be vested in my widow during her lifetime as sovereign of this principality and mother of the child adopted.' He also referred to the treaty of 1817, which guaranteed the throne to the maharaja and 'his heirs and successors'. Ellis assured him 'that he would do everything possible'.

Two days later, on 21 November 1853, Gangadhar Rao breathed his last. He was allowed to die under the delusion that his fidelity to the British would be remembered. But the despot at the Government House in Calcutta had other designs.

Lakshmi Bai became a widow at the age of twenty-five.After the maharaja's death, she was at a decisive turning point, both in her personal life as well as in her role as the rani. She faced these dual crises with guts and intelligence. She had been widowed at a young age and she was childless. There is no doubt that she had been very fond of her stern but sensitive husband, although he was much older than her. She went through all the elaborate rituals associated with a husband's death and observed the thirteen-day period of mourning. But she did not go through the distasteful and disfiguring ritual of having her head shaved, which widows were expected to do. The Rani next threw away the veil and came out of purdah. This was a startlingly bold development and, again, defied tradition. But the Rani had a purpose. She felt that if she was to mean anything to her people she must be much more than a veiled shadow in the background. At this time, they needed a leader who was accessible, a leader whom they could see and talk to. The last thing they needed was an intangible shrouded presence. The Rani, however, continued to maintain strict purdah in her dealings with British officials. She would not allow foreigners the familiarity of seeing her openly. She talked to them from behind a screen and her attitude with them was stiff yet correct.

After she gave up purdah, she began to go on horseback through the streets of Jhansi, clad in a Maratha-style sari. Her entourage included some of her *sardar*s and a few soldiers in Maratha uniforms. The people greeted her warmly whenever they saw her. She also started receiving her subjects every day at a durbar at the palace where she provided them with help and guidance. Meadows Taylor, a British writer, says, 'She had no affectations of personal concealment; and she sat daily on the throne of her deceased husband, hearing reports, giving directions, hearing petitions and comporting herself as a brave-minded woman had to do in her position.'

In her role as rani, she set about the task of administering the state. She was no novice and over several years, at Gangadhar's suggestion, she had involved herself with matters of state and government and had regular dealings with the *diwan* and other senior state officials. But now, after Gangadhar's death, she was maneuvering in a difficult situation. She had not been proclaimed the Rani as yet and her administrative freedom was restricted. The Jhansi army had not been disbanded and was under her control. On the other hand, the British had taken over the treasury and sealed the prisons.

The Rani had carefully thought out her actions. First, she wanted to show the British that she was more than capable of governing the state. Next, if the succession issue went in her favour, getting closer to her subjects was the right starting point. And finally, if the British decided against her, she needed the people even more.

One cannot help wondering what this extraordinary woman looked like. There are some portraits of the Rani done by contemporary artists. One of these remarkable paintings is at the Victoria and Albert Museum in London and shows a young Lakshmi Bai dressed in fine clothes and wearing her fabulous pearls and diamonds. Along with *kan phool* (long earrings), she wears above her forehead a jeweled *kalgi* (aigrette). The face is oval, the eyes large and luminous and the nose delicate and finely chiseled. Altogether, a very beautiful woman!

A pen picture has been given by the writer Medows Taylor:

> In appearance she was fair and handsome, with a noble presence and figure and a dignified and resolute, indeed stern expression, which appeared to have usurped the place of the peculiar softness which, when she was younger and had a good hope of a prosperous life, had distinguished her ... Her dress, though that of a woman, was not the ordinary costume generally worn by females of her class and position in life. On her head she had a small cap of bright-coloured scarlet silk with a string of pearls and rubies encircling and laced into it, and round her neck a diamond necklace sparkled, of not less value than a lakh of rupees, at least. Her bodice, freely open in front, showed a well-developed, voluptuous bust and terminated at the waist, which was somewhat tightly drawn in by a belt worked over and embroidered with gold, and in it were ostentatiously stuck two elaborately carved silver-mounted pistols of Damascus make, together with a small but elegantly shaped hand-dagger, the point of which, it was whispered, had been dipped in a subtle poison whereby a wound, however, slight, must prove fatal. Instead of the usual cloth or petticoat, she wore a pair of loose trousers, from which protruded her small, prettily rounded bare feet.

Sir John Smythe in *The Rebellious Rani* quotes the historical records of the 14th Kings Hussars, which have this to say about the Rani. 'She was a very handsome woman, about twenty-four years of age, a perfect Amazon in bravery, leading her troops, mounted like a man just the sort of daredevil woman that soldiers admire.'

British writers often dwell on 300 years of British rule in India. This is manifestly not true. For much of this period, they were in

India as obsequious and lowly traders and not as rulers. It was not a case of outright conquest of one country by another, but a story of slow penetration, in which the people of the land themselves helped the foreign intruder. By the early 1800s, they held about one-third of the country, mainly in south and eastern India. After this, the Marathas who were the major power in India, fought till 1818 and the Sikhs till 1849.

It was during the time that Lord Dalhousie was governor general that a stupendous growth took place with regard to British territory in India. Dalhousie annexed several Indian states under the policy of lapse, whereby on the failure to produce natural heirs, the sovereignty of the 'dependent' states lapsed to the British government. It also did not acknowledge the right of those states to adopt heirs. Eight Indian states, whose rulers had died without leaving a linear heir, were annexed during Dalhousie's regime.

Dalhousie's policy led to a strong sense of insecurity and injustice among the rulers of various Indian states. Many discontented princes, expropriated landlords and their followers and retainers were thus driven to join the revolt. Lord Dalhousie can, in that sense, be labelled the chief instigator of the revolt of 1857.

Although Major Ellis, the assistant political agent at Jhansi and his superior, D.A. Malcolm located at Gwalior, both recommended that the adopted son be recognized as heir, Dalhousie sitting in the Government House in Calcutta, would not agree. The Rani did not wait for any pronouncement from Calcutta but took the initiative and wrote to Dalhousie in December 1853, seeking the government's acknowledgement of the adoption. She referred to the three treaties with the British and stressed the fact that clause two of the treaty of 1817 clearly stated that adopted sons would be acknowledged as heirs and successors. She also described in detail the formalities scrupulously observed at her son's adoption and the presence of Ellis and his colleague at her husband's request.

She made the important point that adoptions made by the three neighbouring states of Datia, Orchha, and Jalaun had been sanctioned by the government and asked how the privilege of adoption could be denied to Jhansi when it was allowed to the others.

In the drawing up of these documents, she took the help of her ministers, but none of them had any legal training or background. She is said to have written the documents herself in Persian. In the drafting, one can see her clear thinking and logic, and cannot help being amazed at the many talents of this young woman.

Dalhousie, however, had the last word, at least till 1857. He turned down the Rani's plea and decided to annex the state. He advanced several pseudo legal arguments in support of this, but these were clearly flawed and misleading. The historian, Sir John Kaye, judged Jhansi as 'the worst of Dalhousie's annexation'.

With regard to the precedents quoted by the Rani, where adoption in the three neighbouring states was recognized, he made the most astonishing and biased statement 'that a concession by the British government of the privileges to adopt on any particular occasion from motives of friendship or policy by no means involves the admission of a right to adopt on the part of any other state.'

Dalhousie summarily instructed D.A. Malcolm, Political Agent at Gwalior, to take steps to take possession of Jhansi as a British territory. He wrote, 'As Jhansi lies in the midst of other British districts, the possession of it as our own will tend to the improvement of the general internal administration of our possessions of Bundelkhand.' Town criers went round the various towns and villages of the state announcing the takeover. It was indeed a black day for the people of Jhansi. They had always believed that the adoption of Damodar would be recognized and till he came of age, their beloved Rani would continue to guide their destinies.

Ellis, who had always been sympathetic to the Jhansi royal family, was given the embarrassing task of reading the proclamation to the Rani. According to an eyewitness account, the Rani is believed to have received the agent of Lord Dalhousie most courteously but separated by purdah. When the British representative informed her of the heart-rending news that Jhansi thenceforth ceased to belong to her, that it had been incorporated with the domains of the English, 'Luchmee Bai', in a loud yet melodious voice, replied to the agent of the English in these significant words, '*Meri Jhansi nahin dungi*!' (I will not surrender my Jhansi!)

The Rani left the meeting with Ellis in bitter fury. Some of her women companions and attendants were in tears and asked, 'Rani Sahiba, what will happen now?' She told them, 'Whatever happens, the Rani of Jhansi was not born to shed tears.' Brave words, but what indeed could she do? She paced the palace in despair. She was a Hindu widow, faced with a hopeless future. A ruler who had lost her throne. A mother with her son's hopes of succession shattered. A woman whose dreams were destroyed.

The Rani could not reconcile herself to the government's decision and a month after the proclamation, she wrote yet again to Dalhousie and also sent her attorney Kashmiri Mull to Calcutta. She added that her case had been decided in the absence of her representative, while even trifling cases could only be decided in the presence of the parties concerned.

After she had persisted in sending yet another petition in June 1854, came the governor general's abrupt reply. It did not deal with the points raised by the Rani in her various appeals but asserted that the case had been 'long and deliberately discussed by Governor-General in Council and no valid argument had been presented for altering the just and reasonable decision the Government of India was led to form.' She refused to accept this reply and wrote again in July, mentioning that the dispossession constituted a violation of treaties and 'it must involve gross violation and negation of British faith and honour'. More significantly, she pointed out that the decision regarding Jhansi had 'created great disquietude among the native princes and chiefs of Upper India'.

By now, she was losing hope of ever getting justice from the British, but decided that the only way was to send a mission to London. This included the Rani's attorney, Kashmiri Mull, and an Englishman, and it cost her sixty thousand rupees. The mission presented her appeal to the Court of Directors in London in which she brought to bear the full facts of her case and the total injustice that had been done to her and her people. The appeal fell on ears deaf to all considerations, except those of immediate material gain. Her case was finally lost and Dalhousie's word became law.

The British authorities had made decisions regarding the provisions that had to be made for her future. D.A. Malcolm had recommended to the governor general that a pension of five thousand rupees per month be given to the Rani during her lifetime. She was, however, to vacate the main palace in the fort and move to another palace in the city. The latter would be considered her private property. All other state buildings were deemed to have lapsed, along with the state. She and her retinue were to be exempt from arrest and were not subject to the jurisdiction of British courts. It was further recommended that in compliance with her husband's request, all state jewels, private funds and the balance remaining in the public treasury should be considered her private property. Unsympathetic as Dalhousie was to the Rani, he approved these proposals except the one relating to the state jewels and private funds. The Rani refused to accept the pension or the property willed to Damodar as it was stipulated that certain debts incurred by the last Maharaja should be deducted from the pension and the private property. According to the historian Malleson, this action 'added meanness to insult'.

The Rani quietly left the royal palace in the fort and moved to the City Palace. She felt that she had been disgraced and was 'looked down upon' by the neighbouring chiefs of Bundelkhand. John Lang, her legal counsel, had at one stage advised her not to do anything rash, as a wing of a native regiment and some artillery were within three marches of the palace and that she could be destroyed. She had taken the advice, but deep inside her was an unrelenting determination to retrieve her state. She was reported to have said, 'I will draw my sword, but only when it will be most effective. I will not draw it in vain.'

The British made the necessary administrative arrangements in Jhansi. The Jhansi State army was disbanded and units of the Bengal army under British officers now garrisoned the fort. In addition, a battalion of Scindia's Gwalior Contingent was posted to Jhansi and part of this battalion also garrisoned the Kerrera fort, which was another stronghold of the state. The cannons on the ramparts of Jhansi fort were rendered unusable and other weapons were confiscated. A Political Officer, Captain Skene, was appointed to administer the state.

Captain Skene found that 'the minds of the inhabitants were unsettled', what further fuelled the people's hatred for the British was their worsening economic situation. The administrative set-up of the Maharaja was dismantled by the British as a result of which several people became unemployed. The Jhansi army had already been disbanded and the soldiers were rendered idle. The cumulative effect of all these measures was that the economy of Jhansi suffered, adding to the woes of the people. John Sullivan wrote, 'With the disappearance of the native court, trade languishes, the capital decays and the people are impoverished. The Englishman flourishes and acts like a sponge, drawing up riches from the banks of the Ganges and squeezing them down upon the banks of the Thames.'

Another measure, which was particularly galling to the Rani, as to all Hindus, was the introduction of cow slaughter in Jhansi, which had been earlier prohibited. Further offence was given to the Rani and the people by British measures relating to the beautiful Mahalakshmi temple. The maharaja had granted in perpetuity two villages to this temple and the revenues were used for its upkeep. The British ruled that these two villages must be resumed along with the rest of the state. This would have dire consequences for the temple. But the Rani's protests were in vain.

Meanwhile, the Rani continued her daily rides into the town and met the people in the streets and gardens of Jhansi. Her subjects continued to nurse the secret hope that she might yet provide an alternative to British rule. The Rani also kept up her daily routine of strenuous physical exercise, which included some intensive practice with *mukdar* (Indian clubs). She also trained long hours with weapons. Her skill with the sword was particularly good and spoken of with admiration by expert swordsmen.

She kept abreast of all the happenings in Jhansi and the other states of Bundelkhand. The Rani also had some agents operating in the cantonment. One of these was Moti Bai, who had been a prominent performer in the theatre patronized by the late maharaja. She and another companion sang *bhajan*s to the sipahis of the British contingent. They also gleaned much information, which was passed on to the Rani. She learnt about the discontent among the sipahis, the intolerance and incompetence of some of the British officers, and the happenings in other British army stations. Moti Bai was a brave and loyal woman. She and her companion, Jalkhari Dulaiya, distinguished themselves during the British siege of Jhansi and both were finally killed in the hand-to-hand fighting that followed the enemy's entry to the fort.

When her son was seven years old, Rani Lakshmi Bai planned his thread ceremony, which was held with much pomp. At this function, the Rani met several of her friends from Bithur, including Tatya Tope. They discussed the discontent of the sipahis in the Bengal army and the rumblings all over the Awadh area. They also decided to maintain contact with each other and with the other centres of national discontent.

By June 1857, the rebels had liberated Delhi and the surrounding areas, as well as the recently annexed kingdom of Awadh, and its capital Lucknow with the exception of the Residency where the British were besieged. This vast tract of liberated territory was not far from Jhansi. Within Bundelkhand itself there was general unrest and disorder. Several Rajput chiefs including Raja Mardan Singh of Banpur had broken into rebellion.

Jhansi was garrisoned by the 12th Native Infantry of the Bengal army together with detachments of artillery and cavalry. Captain A. Skene was the political officer in charge of the state and Captain Dunlop commanded the garrison. When news of the revolt at Meerut reached Jhansi in May 1857, Skene wrote, 'There is, of course, a great feeling of uneasiness and the Thakurs (Rajput landowners) are beginning to talk of doing something.'

On 1 June, two bungalows in the military cantonment were burnt down. This was a signal in many districts that the sipahis were ready and poised for revolt. However, neither Skene nor Dunlop took any precautions. On 6 June, a company of the Native Infantry led by a sergeant, Gurbaksh Singh, raised the flag of rebellion and marched into a small fort in the cantonment, called Star Fort, which contained the magazine and the treasury. As they marched to her fort, the citizens of Jhansi cheered and showered them with flowers and garlands.

Skene ordered all seventy British or Anglo Indian residents to move to the City Fort immediately. Express messages were also sent to Gwalior and Kanpur asking for help, though it did not seem likely that any help would be forthcoming. Before long all the troops joined the mutiny. They then marched to the jail and released all prisoners and the jail *darogah,* Bakshish Ali, along with his guards joined the troops. The sipahis next killed Dunlop and all other British officers in the cantonment.

Vishnu Godse says that Captain Gordon and some others then appealed to Lakshmi Bai, the woman they had so grievously wronged, to take charge of the kingdom and save their lives. Godse quotes the Rani's cold response, 'You took my kingdom from me under false pretences and now that you cannot keep it, you hand it back to me and ask for my help. My case was decided against me without giving me a hearing. If I now give you any protection, the rebel *sipahi*s will destroy me. You have to look after yourselves and save your lives any way you can.' The Rani, however, agreed to shelter the European women and children; this was the most she could do, considering her own vulnerable position.

On 7 June, the sipahis laid siege to the City Fort where all the foreigners had taken refuge. The rebel gunners then brought up two cannons to the fort walls and Captain Skene decided to surrender. The gates were thrown open and the English and Anglo-Indian men, women and children filed out, but they were immediately taken prisoners.

They were then led in a procession through the city to an area called Jokhan Bagh beyond the city wall, where the crowd kept shouting, '*Firangi Ko Maro*' (Kill the foreigners). A message then arrived from the leader of the Jhansi mutiny, *rissaldar* Kale Khan, ordering that all Europeans should be put to death. A general massacre took place led by Bakshish Ali, the jail *darogah,* who first shot down Captain Skene. The total number of people killed was over sixty.

The massacre at Jhansi was horrible. However, it must be understood that there was much brutality on both sides. By the time the revolt spread to Jhansi, the rebels had been taught a lesson in savagery by their enemies. In May 1857, Colonel James Neill, arrived in Benares with the 1st Madras European Fusiliers and unleashed the most hideous terror in the province. Colonel Neill's 'hangings' became notorious. There were hundreds of others as diabolical as Neill, massacring old men and helpless women. The British were bent on settling scores making up for one life by taking fifty. To kill an Indian became the 'best sport'. One of the most gruesome punishments adopted by the British was the blowing away of rebels from the mouths of cannons.

There has been controversy regarding the Rani's precise role in the mutiny and massacre at Jhansi. Contemporary English historians such as Kaye, Malleson, and Forest maintain that the Rani instigated the mutiny at Jhansi and caused the massacre of the English. They hold her responsible because 'her perceptions of real and fancied wrongs inspired in her a smoldering hatred of the British race'.

Later, Indian and English historians re-examined this evidence in depth. They also studied the extensive historical records at the National Achives in New Delhi and the Library of the India Office in London. The long time that has elapsed since the mutiny enabled these scholars to have a more detached view and eliminate passion and prejudice. As a result, their conclusions are quite different from those of earlier writers.

R.C. Majumdar, the eminent historian, notes that 'as far as the guilt of the Rani is concerned … it is not a little curious that while the historians felt no hesitation in accepting the Rani's guilt as definitely proved by the incriminating statements of these witnesses, they never alluded to the points in her favour. Nor do they seem to have considered the evidence collected by Sir Robert Hamilton in April 1858.'

Sir Robert Hamilton had long been associated with central India as agent to the governor general and had met the Rani on several occasions. He says, 'Not a paper incriminating the Ranee did I find nor did there appear any evidence that she desired or was privy to the murder of any Europeans … The English were induced to leave the fort by the persuasion of the *Darogah* of the jail and a *Rissaldar* of the Irregulars. The Rani was not present or any man on her part.'

In fact, the Rani's own position at this confused time was precarious. If she had given full support to the British, she would have been killed by the rebels; while if she had given succour to the rebels, the British would have been after her blood. The offer of shelter to the women and children, which Godse says she made when Gordon and some others appealed to her for help, was as much as she could realistically do.

Finally, anyone who has seriously studied the life of the Rani will understand that it would have been totally out of character for her to be involved with the massacre of women and children. She was a chivalrous and caring person. While she was in touch with rebel leaders in Bundelkhand, and to that extent was involved in the revolt, she could by no stretch of imagination have been involved in the murder of innocents.

The sequence of events that followed the massacre of the Europeans was that *rissaldar* Kale Khan, the ringleader of the mutineers in Jhansi, decided to march with the men to Delhi, which was 390 kilometres away. The mutineers also issued a proclamation that 'The people are God's, the country is the King's and the two religions govern.'

Delhi was the centre of the revolt and Bahadur Shah sat on the Mughal throne. Soldiers who had mutinied in the surrounding military stations were all converging at Delhi. The *sipahi*s at Jhansi were, however, short of funds. They, therefore, went to the palace of the Rani with loaded guns and demanded three hundred thousand rupees in cash and supplies of ammunition and guns. They surrounded the palace and their leaders threatened to blow up the building, laying a trail of gunpowder to underline the threat. Their argument was simple: they had rid Jhansi of the British, therefore they must be rewarded.

The Rani was in a precarious position because any help to the *sipahi*s would ultimately result in a clash with the British, which she wanted to avoid. Meanwhile, the rebels, in order to increase the pressure on the Rani, invited Sadashiv Rao to take over the government at Jhansi. Sadashiv Rao was a distant relation of Maharaja Gangadhar Rao and the *sipahi*s were using him as a pawn in their negotiations with the Rani.

Under this dual threat from the soldiers, the Rani used all her guile. She told them, 'You know very well that my state has been under the British. They have deprived me of my wealth and left me a pittance. My days have been difficult and you are adding to my woes. This is no way for gallant soldiers to treat a helpless woman.' In the subsequent parleys, she got them to agree to scale down their demands and finally agreed to pay them one hundred thousand rupees on condition that they leave Jhansi immediately. The *sipahi*s then gave over the Jhansi territory to her and another proclamation was issued: 'The people are God's, the country is the Badshah's and the Raj is Rani Lakshmi Bai's.'

The Rani now took over the administration of Jhansi as no other authority existed. As the *bhagwa jhanda* (orange flag) of the Marathas was hoisted on all the state buildings, the people were jubilant. They collected in large numbers at her palace and hailed her as their Maharani.

Administering the state was no simple matter as no organization existed. The older set-up had been dismantled by the British. The experienced state officials had left Jhansi and taken up employment in other states of Bundelkhand. To add to the chaos, the sipahis had burnt down the administration offices in the city and all the public records and documents essential to any government.

The Rani was not an experienced administrator, but she was highly intelligent and learnt fast as she went along. Her top advisors included Moropant Tambe, Diwan Jawahar Singh, Raghuanth Singh, Lallu Bakshi, Diwan Lachman Rao and others. They were devoted men but lacked her vision and determination. The main responsibility for formulating policies fell on her. After having taken control of Jhansi, the Rani set about mending her fences with the British. The rebels left for Delhi on 12 June 1857 and that very day, she sent a letter to Major Erskine, commissioner, Sagar Division, informing him that the government's sipahis had killed all the Europeans. She had no resources to make arrangements for the safety of the district but had saved the town of Jhansi from being plundered. She needed funds and competent government forces to run the district and promised to await further instructions.

Major Erskine, who replied on 2 July, did not doubt the Rani's sincerity. He wrote, 'Until a new Superintendent arrives at Jhansi,

I beg you will manage the district for the British government, collecting the revenue, raising such police as may be necessary, and making other proper arrangements such as you know government will approve, and when the Superintendent takes charge from you, he will not only give you no trouble but will repay you for all your losses and expenses and deal liberally with you.'

The governor general, who was already biased against the Rani, only accorded a conditional approval to Erskine's action. By this time, the Rani had already assumed the administration of the state though she was aware of the insecurity of her position. Her agents in Major Erskine's office told her of the commissioner's correspondence with Calcutta, which made plain to her what to expect from the British when they returned to Jhansi. They were obviously not prepared to hear her side of the story and were going to condemn her for the mutiny at Jhansi.

Lakshmi Bai's first priority was to re-establish law and order. Dacoits were plundering villages and terrorizing people in the area around Barwa Sagar, a town a few kilometres from the capital. The Rani went and camped there, personally participated in the raids, destroyed gangs and saw them hung or sentenced.

Her second priority was to prepare herself for the coming confrontation with the British. For this purpose, she started organizing and equipping an army. At the same time, knowing that she could not stand alone against them, she set about strengthening her contacts with centres of national discontent in order to join hands with them at the opportune moment.

In a few months, she had the administration going smoothly. New public offices were built to replace those burnt down, law courts started functioning, the police operated efficiently and there were no serious crimes in the state and her own money was minted. She took a lot of interest in adding to and improving the state library, which had been started by her late husband. She was fond of classical music and patronized sitar players and other musicians from Gwalior, which was an important centre for classical music. The Jhansi theatre, her late husband's absorbing interest, was also supported.

During these days the Rani would get up at five in the morning. The first thing she did was to exercise in the gymnasium. She spent an hour or two every day practicing with Indian clubs and honing her skills with the sword, wrestling and horse riding. She would then take a bath with fragrant attar and wear a *chanderi* sari of faultless white. She would next sit down for her daily prayers and worship with the court musicians providing the music for the puja. Later in the morning, the *sardar*s and other state officials came to pay their respects. There were 150 of them and even if one of them failed to turn up, her keen eye would notice the absence and the next time they came, she would ask the reason for it. After lunch, she would take an hour's rest, unless there was some urgent work. At three in the afternoon, she held the durbar. For this function she usually wore male attire, which consisted of Jodhpur breeches, a blue silk jacket and turban. A sash went round her waist in which she carried a sword, the hilt and scabbard of which were embellished with rubies. She was tall and beautiful and her attire added to her already impressive presence. Occasionally for the durbar, she opted for conventional garments and wore a white sari with several strings of pearls round her neck and diamond-studded bangles and rings. She sat on a *gaddi* (throne), flanked by two attendants bearing maces damascened in gold and silver. At the durbar, Diwan Lakshman Rao, the chief minister, presented the relevant document to her, which she quickly scanned and issued clear and precise orders.

Twice a week, the Rani and her son went in procession to the Mahalakshmi temple, with its lake filled with lotus flowers. Sometimes she went on horseback and at other times in a palanquin decorated with curtains and gold brocade. At the head of the procession were a drummer and a flag-bearer, while the rear was taken up by a mounted escort of soldiers in Maratha uniforms. A further touch of glamour was added by her beautifully-attired handmaidens who walked alongside her palanquin.

Godse says that one cold wintry evening, while returning from the temple, she saw the poor of the town in coarse cotton garments huddling around hastily-built fires in the bylanes of the city. She got down from the palanquin and asked them all to come to her palace in four days' time. All the tailors of the town were kept very busy for those four days. When the poor in their hundreds gathered in front of the palaces, every one of them was handed over a woolen jacket, cap and a blanket.

The first challenge to Rani Lakshmi Bai's authority at Jhansi came from an unexpected source. Sadashiv Rao, finding his claim to the Jhansi throne ignored by the rebels, collected a few thousand men and captured the Kurrera fort about fifty kilometres from the capital. He thought that in the prevailing anarchy, his time had come and he declared himself the maharaja of Jhansi and pillaged and plundered the surrounding villages. The Rani sent a body of men under Jawahar Singh, who captured the impostor and lodged him at the Jhansi fort as a state prisoner.

The Rani's troubles were not over. The challenge next time came from the neighbouring states of Orchha and Datia. The Rajputs of Bundelkhand regarded the Marathas as interlopers in their region. Larai Rani (Warrior Queen) who ruled Orchha saw her chance of regaining the territory lost to Jhansi. The British had collapsed and Rani Lakshmi Bai was unprepared for war. Larai Rani was joined by the neighbouring state of Datia and their combined forces totaling twenty-five thousand were placed under the command of her Diwan, Nathe Khan. He sent word to the Rani to surrender. To which her reply was: 'Do your worst. I will make a woman out of you.'

Lakshmi Bai had few troops and her military stores were poor. Some advisors suggested arriving on a truce but she shamed them all by declaring, 'You are not manly enough to fight, but I, a woman, will teach you how to take on the enemy.'

She then summoned her *sardar*s, among whom were Diwan Jawahar Singh and Raghunath Singh Nauner. She appealed to them for help with militia and horse. They rallied around and said that with the British thrown out of the state, Jhansi was once again independent and it was their bounden duty to help defend it. In a few days, Jhansi became a vast camp of military leaders, with their men all eagerly waiting for the clash of steel and the smoke of battle. Mardan Singh, the Raja of the neighbouring state of Banpur, allied himself with the Rani and came with badly-needed provisions and cannons.

When news came that Nathe Khan was on the move, Lakshmi Bai assembled her noblemen and fully armed, rode in front of the militia taking their salute. She then summoned Diwan Jawahar Singh who was a Parmar Rajput and the *jagirdar* of a nearby village. She tied an orange string round his wrist, thus entrusting the nobleman with the command of the army and honouring him in the presence of all his peers and the militia. Diwan Jawahar Singh placed his sword at the Rani's feet to show his allegiance to her.

Aware of his strength, the Rani let Nateh Khan advance without opposition till he was within range of her cannons on the ramparts of Jhansi fort. The Orchha army thinking that it would be an easy victory as they had not been opposed, advanced recklessly towards the city. The Rani's artillery, under the command of the redoubtable Gulam Ghaus Khan, now opened an intense fire, forcing the invaders to fall back. Nathe Khan decided to be more circumspect and started to concentrate his fire at the six gates of the city with a view to smashing them down and entering the city where the greater strength of his army would be a deciding factor. The Orchha gate suffered heavy damage and there was the fear that it might give way. The Rani was constantly at this gate, exposed to the enemy's fire, but her very presence at this vulnerable point was a great inspiration to her men. The damage was repaired and the gate stood. The siege went on for twenty days. The Rani's biggest gun, *Kadak Bijli*, with its greater range, played havoc in the enemy ranks and Nathe Khan's guns were finally silenced and he was forced to withdraw. Jawahar Singh and Raghunath Singh with a large body of cavalry pursued the retreating forces and inflicted heavy damages. Rani Lakshmi Bai's crushing victory forced Larai Rani to sue for peace. Lakshmi Bai demanded war damages and once this was paid, she behaved generously towards her fellow queen.

The victory over the Datia and Orchha forces raised the Rani's prestige all over Bundelkhand and the neighbouring states viewed her with newfound respect. In Jhansi, the personal regard for her was now sky high. As we see in this battle and the several subsequent battles against the British, the Rani believed in leading by example. She fought alongside her men and was usually where the greatest danger lay. No wonder the men followed her wherever she led them.

Rani Lakshmi Bai had long known that despite her efforts to the contrary, a showdown with the British was inevitable. Consequently, during the peace and tranquility that followed her destruction of the forces of Orchha and Datia, she did not give up her military preparations.

She re-enlisted in her army all the soldiers from the old Jhansi army, which numbered about 5,000 men and that had been disbanded by the British. She then called for volunteers from all over the state. The response was splendid and she raised a force that was estimated at 10,000 to 11,000 men. The majority of these were Bundelas, but also included 1,500 rebel sipahis trained in the Company's army. She also had about 1,000 Afghans who, although mercenaries, were fiercely loyal to her. Always unorthodox in whatever she did, she did not make the slightest distinction between Hindus, Muslim or soldiers of any other caste. These troops were trained intensively and the Rani personally supervised their daily military exercises and drill.

Her special interest had always been the induction of women as soldiers, another facet of her unorthodox approach. They were taught to ride, shoot, fence and to serve cannon. Several of these women soldiers were later killed on the ramparts of the fort and many more died during the hand-to-hand fighting in the streets of Jhansi.

Diwan Jawahar Singh, who had proved his worth in the earlier engagement against Orchha and Datia, remained in command. He was supported by Diwan Raghunath Singh of Nauner. The guns were in charge of her famous gunner, Gulam Ghaus Khan, an Afghan mercenary.

After the British had annexed Jhansi, one of the first things they did was to destroy the guns or make them unusable and bury them under garbage. The Rani asked Khuda Buksh, another great gunner, to salvage as many old guns as possible. She also set up foundries to cast new guns. Ammunition and gunpowder was manufactured in large quantities and stored. She also set up factories for the manufacture of rifles, pistols, swords, and spears.

Her two great cannons were *Bhawani Shankar*, made at Orchha by the famous Jairam, and *Karak Bijli*, with its mouth shaped like a lion's. They still stand on the ramparts of the Jhansi fort. By the time the siege started, she had about thirty-five guns. Interestingly, in the National Archives, there are intelligence reports by Sir Robert Hamilton, agent to the governor general for central India, which detail all her war preparations..

Lakshmi Bai had already established contact with other centres of national discontent. She was in touch with rebel leaders at Kalpi and elsewhere. She had contacted Tatya Tope, Mardan Singh, the Raja of Banpur, and the Raja of Shahgarh, who had rendered invaluable assistance to her in her recent battle against Orchha and Datia, sending men and arms.

Although Lakshmi Bai was making these preparations for war, she kept up her efforts to placate the British. However, she was getting disillusioned and exasperated by their indifference to her appeals. The Rani had realized that the British intended to make her a scapegoat for the mutiny and even the massacre. Jhansi had to be avenged and the victim had to be a person of sufficient importance.

While there was peace in Jhansi from August 1857 to February 1858, most of the country around was aflame and battles raged. By 21 September 1857, Delhi had been reoccupied. The loss of Delhi deprived the insurgents of an important rallying point.

After the British had conquered Upper India again, they could afford to turn their attention to the last stronghold of the revolt: central India and Jhansi in particular. By now the British were in a much stronger position with regard to men and equipment. A lot of time and effort was spent by them in order to assemble the Central India Field Force at Mhow and Sehore, which contained seasoned troops, rushed from Britain, and hand-picked Indians. This was a considerable force and included regiments of cavalry, infantry, and artillery. Its strongest arm was the artillery, which would be most effective against the strength of the Jhansi fortifications, as well the several fortresses en route.

Lord Canning, the new governor general, deemed the Rani of Jhansi – 'the Jezebel of India' – a serious threat and a focal point for the rebels of central India and therefore, selected a seasoned general to pit against her. This man was General Sir Hugh Rose, who although new to India, was one of the most distinguished generals of the British army. He later became a Field Marshal and was elevated to the peerage as Lord Straitnairn. By now Rose was fifty-seven years old, but he was still a formidable adversary supported by a strong and experienced army. While on the march from Mhow to Jhansi, Rose was attacked by Mardan Singh, the Raja of Banpur. Although his attack was well planned, the Raja failed in his attempt. Soon after, Mardan Singh made a second resolute stand at Barodia in an effort to deny passage to the British across the Bina River. In this battle, casualties among the British were high, but after the Raja was wounded and many of his officers killed, he had to abandon his position.

Sir Hugh Rose marched on towards Jhansi, staying at Sagar for a month. He collected goats, sheep, oxen, grain, flour and large supplies of tea. Stocks of beer, soda water and wine were also laid in, enabling the Parsi shopkeepers of Sagar to do good business. He added guns, howitzers, large mortars and ammunition from the Sagar arsenal. Some of the guns were so large and heavy that Rose had to get an additional number of elephants to carry them.

Sir Hugh Rose had to cross some mountain passes en route to Jhansi. These were defended by the gallant rajas of Banpur and Shahgarh. The engagement at the Nurat pass was considered by Rose to he the most critical of the campaign so far. The pass forms a narrow gorge between two ranges of hills thickly covered with jungle. The Raja of Shahgarh planted cannons on both sides of the gorge. He had also concealed skirmishers in the jungle who would be able to harass the advancing enemy. As the British began to ascend into the pass, the Raja's guns opened fire and the hills seemed alive with his infantry. The British drove back the Raja's infantry but so heavy was the fire from his artillery that the British advance was checked and Rose gave the order for the guns to fall back. The artillery men were forced to take refuge behind the guns. The Raja's fire increased in intensity and Rose late described it 'as rapid and hot a fire as ever I saw'. The numbers of those killed and wounded increased every moment. General Rose had his horse shot under him and barely escaped with his life. The setback was, however, only temporary because Rose had the heavier artillery.

The guns of the Hyderabad Contingent came up at this moment and their counter-shelling was followed by a charge by the Purabias of this contingent, supported by the 3rd Europeans. This pushed back the Raja's forces and after some intense hand-to-hand fighting, forced him to withdraw. This lost battle had a demoralizing effect on the rebels, although skirmishing by rebel troops continued all the way to Jhansi.

Lakshmi Bai had been carefully watching the British movement from central India towards Jhansi. Her agents had informed her that the British force had been detained at Sagar for want of supplies and transport. In order to make it more difficult for the enemy to collect supplies, Lakshmi Bai cleverly laid waste the countryside around Jhansi; all grass, firewood, vegetables were burnt or moved inside the city. To deny cover to the enemy, trees were cut down, walls and other shelters dismantled. This could have caused considerable embarrassment to the besiegers, but Scindia of Gwalior and the Rani of Orchha came to the rescue and kept the British force abundantly supplied throughout the operation.

Along with her army chief, Jawahar Singh, and the chief gunner, Gulam Ghaus Khan, the Rani supervised the building of new gun sites and had the existing ones strengthened. She also organized a fire brigade in anticipation of bombardment. As Brigadier Sir John Smyth in the *Rebellious Rani* says, 'How this well brought up Hindu lady could have learned so much of the fundamentals of war is one of the mysteries which shroud her personality. Like Joan of Arc she had a flair for military leadership and seemed to know instinctively the right course to pursue better than most of the other more experienced rebel leaders.' Joan of Arc had her voices, Lakshmi Bai simply had a natural wisdom in these matters.

During the weeks before the British forces' arrival at Jhansi, Rani Lakshmi Bai, in addition to making preparations for war, also kept writing letters to Sir Robert Hamilton and Commissioner W.C. Erskine, in the hope that they would accept her assurance of loyalty and she would be able to avoid war. But this was not to be.

On 15 March, five days before the enemy arrived, Mardan Singh, Raja of Banpur and the Raja of Shahgarh rode into Jhansi. The former brought his son Sher Singh and 2,500 infantry and cavalry, and two guns. Another round of consultations was held but there was no consensus on whether or not to go to war. The two rajas then left for Kalpi to join Tatya Tope.

After these consultations, Lakshmi Bai finally resolved to fight and she knew it would be a fight to death. Once she made up her mind, she did not waver for an instant. 'To submit was to court dishonour, to fight was to save honour, though everything else might be lost.' She also got the welcome news that Tatya Tope was on the move and was advancing to her aid with a force of 20,000 men.

She assembled her soldiers, townsmen and elders of Jhansi in a town square. There she appeared on a war elephant, dressed like a man and fully armed, with her son, Damodar, sitting by her side. She gave a stirring speech from the *howda* of the elephant, a gist of which is:

> My beloved brothers and sisters. The insolent foreigners have dared to set foot on our sacred soil. Do not be downcast but be of good heart. We fight for what is just and we have made all the preparations for war. Jhansi will teach the English a lesson they will never forget. Tatya Tope, who has already made their General Windham bite the dust at Kanpur, is on the march. He and the Rajas of Banpur and Shahgarh have promised us generous help in men, guns and ammunition. We will be free and independent if we are victorious, if defeated and slain on the battle field we will have eternal glory.

The people burst into tumultuous cheer and cries of 'Rani Lakshmi Bai ki Jai' and 'Jhansi Raj ki Jai'. The enthusiasm of the people to fight to death for the freedom of Jhansi was immense.

Lakshmi Bai had sent an appeal for help to her old friends Tatya Tope and Rao Saheb, who were waiting not far from the borders of her state with large forces. Tatya Tope responded to such effect that he almost upset the British plans. He marched rapidly with a small force of 900 men towards Kalpi and suddenly swooped on the rajas of Panna and Charkhari who were both staunch allies of the British. This put the British authorities into a quandary.

Sir Rose ignored the fall of Charkhari to Tatya Tope and arrived at Jhansi with the Central India Field Force on 20 March 1858. Rose, a proven general and a future field-marshal, was pitted against a thirty-year old woman, who had no experience of modern warfare. The other disparities in their relative strength were manifest in several areas. Though the British army was numerically about equal to the Rani's, it was much superior in terms of equipment, supplies and fire power. It was supported by numerous artillery pieces of varying calibre, sappers and miners, and a siege train. This impressive array was at all events a convincing tribute to Lakshmi Bai.

Rose first completely invested the city and the fortress with his cavalry. He also decided that the capture of the mound or Mamelon, which protected the south side of the fort, was the first and most important operation. It was necessary to concentrate heavy fire on the mound so as to breach the wall and dismantle the defences that protected the mound. The siege then commenced in real earnest. For seventeen long days, the fire from the British batteries and from the defenders of Jhansi was incessant. Shots and shells were poured into the city and the Rani's guns replied powerfully and without respite.

The women and even the children of Jhansi were seen assisting in repairing the defences of the walls and in carrying water and food to the troops on duty. The Rani constantly exposed herself to the enemy's fire and visited troops and inspired them by her presence and her words.

A British intelligence report at army headquarters reads, 'The Chief of the rebel artillery was a first rate gunner, who had under him two companies of *golandaz*. The manner, in which the rebels served their guns, repaired their defenses and reopened fire from batteries and guns repeatedly silenced was remarkable. From some batteries they returned shot for shot. The women were seen working in the batteries and carrying ammunition.' The gunners these reports were referring to were Gulam Ghaus Khan and Khuda Buksh.

Dattatray Balwant Parasnis, the eminent historian who has left a graphic account written in Marathi, says that the enemy continued heavy fire day and night. At night the cannon balls were an awesome sight as they were hurled into the fort glowing like bright-red live coal. He goes on to add that on 26 March, at mid-day, the enemy silenced the guns on the south gate and not a man could make a stand there. Then, Gulam Ghaus Khan, who was on the west gate, swung his guns to the south and his third shot killed the English master gunner and smashed the enemy's guns. Rani Saheba, who was watching through binoculars, was delighted and lavished gifts on Ghaus. That day, there was fierce fighting. The sound was incredible, with soldiers shouting, others crying out in agony, with the thunder of cannons and the volleys of muskets. Trumpets and bugles were sounding everywhere. The air was thick with dust and smoke. Many gunners were killed on the ramparts and others immediately stepped forward to take their place, Rani Saheba was everywhere, she looked to everything, issuing orders and inspiring her men with zeal and enthusiasm.

The British were employing huge siege guns and twenty-four pounders (mortars) and howitzers to cannonade the fort and the mound. The Rani's gunners answered back spiritedly shot for shot. On 21 March, the parapets of the bastion on the mound were damaged and the Rani's guns were silenced for a while. But during the night she had the men and women of Jhansi repair the damages and next morning, the Mamelon was ready for battle once again. As the duel went on day and night, casualties were high among the defenders and were estimated at some sixty to seventy each day. The shelling also damaged many houses and caused extensive fires. The fire brigade was often put into action.

Lakshmi Bai, astride her white charger, was always on the move. She galloped from the city streets to the battlement and back again. In the city, she gave solace to the bereaved and arranged shelter and food for those who had lost their homes. She went from rampart to rampart, from bastion to bastion: she was everywhere, moving her soldiers to where she noticed weaknesses, supervising repair work on city walls and, above all, encouraging and inspiring her troops.

By now, however, she was deeply worried that her friends Rao Saheb and Tatya Tope had not come to her aid. They had promised to move in forces but there was no news of them. Without help how would it all end at Jhansi?

It was now the eleventh day of the siege and the continuous bombardment was taking its toll. The mortars lobbing shells at a high trajectory over the fort walls had devastated the city. Many fires had also been caused in the city because the British had been using cannon balls heated red before firing. This uninterrupted cannonade, as well as the courageous and obstinate defense of Jhansi, had caused a great consumption of British ammunition, so much so that there would not be sufficient ammunition to multiply breaches on the city walls or establish a main breach. Rose had, therefore, decided to assault the place by escalade or ladders and at the same time direct heavy fire on the repaired breach day and night, so that further repair work could not be carried out.

The fortunes of Jhansi were at a low ebb. Rani Lakshmi Bai was anxiously scanning the horizon for Tatya Tope's approaching army. On the evening of 31 March, the lookouts on the tower of the fort glimpsed Tatya's army approaching the Betwa river. A wild shout of joy and exultation went up from the defenders. Lakshmi Bai, Moropant and Jawahar Singh rushed up to the main tower and looking through their binoculars sighted the army as well. Deliverance was at hand.

Tatya Tope's reputation as a great guerrilla leader and general had been enhanced by his recent victories against General Windham at Kanpur. Tatya was an incorrigible optimist. He was defeated in several other battles but the good thing about him was that he never knew when he was beaten, he always came back! On receiving Lakshmi Bai's appeal for help, Tatya tried to disrupt British plans by capturing Charkhari, a staunch ally of the British. He then marched towards Jhansi. But he was to fight under a major handicap. Although his force numbered 15,000 men, a majority of them were raw recruits, with hardly any training. They were equipped with the old slow-firing matchlocks, which could not compare with the Enfield rifles of the *sipahi*s under British command. Details of this battle are given in the chapter on Tatya Tope. The only well-trained troops in his army – the rebel *sipahi*s and the Afghan mercenaries – met the enemy charges most bravely, but were outmaneuvered by Rose's flank attacks. In the continuing battle, Tatya's second line did not hold either, so he set fire to the dry jungle and under cover of the smoke and flames retreated across the Betwa river.

The Battle of Betwa was a disaster, an ignominious defeat. Even accepting that Tatya Tope's troops were untrained and that they were equipped with the outdated matchlocks, the defeat can only be ascribed to Tatya Tope's poor generalship and faulty tactics.

Rani Lakshmi Bai was stunned by Tatya Tope's defeat. She realized that she would have to fight alone. As her difficulties increased, so did her courage and determination to fight. She girded her sword and addressing her troops, said, 'Jhansi looks to nobody for help. We do not need the Peshwa's support; we will rely on our own strength for victory. You have fought bravely and with honour. You are not fighting for your lives but for your honour and honour lies in death. Long after you are dead – and die you must one day – bards will sing your praises and homes will light lamps in your memory. Die then the death of heroes.'

Her troops had absolute faith in her and everyone vowed to fight to the end. Dr Lowe says, 'Their vigilance and their determination to resist abated not one iota; on the contrary, the danger appeared to add to their courage.'

Gulam Ghaus Khan rearranged his guns, Khuda Buksh and other Bundela and Maratha chiefs strengthened their positions and kept up a fearful fire upon the enemy. The Rani went to every post and supervised the defence and both night and day, she was with her men. 'That night,' says Godse of 2 April, 'the British gunners did their best work, their cannonballs super heated and glowing red came over the city and fort like rains in the autumn. Not a soul could get a wink of sleep and danger lurked everywhere. The Rani personally supervised the counter fire. She rewarded the gunners generously and they reopened the silent guns.'

The unceasing fire of the British siege guns had by now damaged the mound or the Mamelon, and the breach became bigger. Rose's plan of attack on Jhansi was to consist of the left attack storming the breach at the mound and the right attack assaulting and mounting the city wall. At three in the morning of 3 April, the British troops moved up to their positions.

The left attack was aided by a traitor in the Rani's camp and although the Jhansi defenders put up a strong opposition, the British managed to force their way in. Parasnis says that the attack would not have succeeded so soon without the help of a traitor, Dulaji Thakar. He was a Bundela Sardar and was in charge of the guns defending the south wall. He not only indicated to the enemy the weakest points in the defence, but also stopped the firing on receiving a signal in order to enable the storming party to force the breach with comparative ease. For these services, the British later rewarded Dulaji with an estate.

The right attack was to mount the walls and this is vividly described by Lowe, who accompanied the British force in his book, *Central India*:

> No sooner did we turn into the road leading towards the gate when the enemy's bugles sounded and a fire of indescribable fierceness opened upon us from the whole line of the wall, and from the towers of the fort overlooking this site. For a time it appeared like a sheet of fire out of which burst a storm of bullets, round shots and rockets, destined for our annihilation. We had upwards of two hundred yards to march through this fiendish fire, and we did it, and the sappers planted the ladders against the wall in three places for the stormers to ascend, but the fire of the enemy waxed stronger and amidst the chaos of sounds of volleys of musketry and roaring of cannons and hissing and bursting of stink pots, infernal machines, huge stones, blocks of wood and trees, all hurried upon their devoted heads, the men wavered for a moment and sheltered themselves behind stones ... Inside bugles were sounding and tom-toms beating madly, while the cannon and the musket were booming and ratting and carrying death among us fast. At this instant, on our right, three of the ladders broke under the weight of men, and a bugle sounded for the Europeans to retire.

It was in this crisis that the British stormers of the left attack, who had already forced the breach at the Mamelon, looked along the wall from the breach and saw the failure of the right attack. They came to the aid of their comrades and charged upon the flank and rear of the Jhansi defenders fighting the right attack.

When the Rani realized that the enemy was inside the city walls in hundreds, for the first time, she showed signs of losing her nerve. But she willed herself to be calm, and soon a terrible anger seized her. At the head of her 1,000 Afghan regulars, she came down from the fort and dashed towards the south wall, a naked sword in hand, and attacked the advancing column of the English. There was fierce hand-to-hand combat, steel clashed against steel, and many, on both sides, were hewn down. The Rani was in the thick of the fight and killed many of the enemy herself. This counter-attack was so ferocious and unexpected that the English fled. They took cover behind pillars, houses and trees and fired from their revolvers. Their losses in fact were heavy and many lay wounded on the street. Godse says, 'Death was flying from house to house with mercurial speed ... Before long the houses on both sides of the street leading to the palace were set on fire.'

The Rani had checked the enemy, but only temporarily. Avoiding a direct fight and having taken cover, the English were directing an intense fire from a distance at the Rani and her men. Bullets were flying everywhere. At this stage, a seventy-five year old Bundela chief, who had accompanied her, realized the danger and pleaded with her to return to the fort. He said, 'If you stay here much longer you will fall prey to the bullets. There are thousands of the enemy in the city because all city gates have been thrown open. It is pointless for you to sacrifice your life. You must return to the fort at once and work out the next step.' The Rani found it difficult to accept this but a moment's reflection showed much sense in it and she returned to the fort to continue the struggle.

Bitter hand-to-hand fighting continued to rage in the streets. Each house and street was tenaciously defended and as the Rani's soldiers retired towards the palace they set fire to the houses. The flames leaped high in the sky and the heat was fearful. The palace had been prepared by the defenders for resistance in the last resort. If the conflict in the streets was severe, at the palace it was desperate. Every room was savagely contested and the Rani's devoted men defended it to the end.

From the fort to which she had returned, Lakshmi Bai could look down at the city where the fighting was still raging. Men, women and children in their hundreds were being burnt to death. Lakshmi Bai was distressed beyond measure and sat down and wept bitter tears. She felt it was because of her that the people were suffering and dying. What right did she have then to live?

She assembled those of her army officers and chiefs who were in the fort and her women companions and retainers and said to them, 'You have fought like tigers for Jhansi but our fate is now sealed. I have brought this suffering upon Jhansi. My people are dying and I have no right to live. The British will never take me alive – even my dead body must not be defiled by their touch. I am going to blow myself up with gunpowder so that no trace is left of me. The rest of you must make your way out of the fort and try and save your lives.'

There was complete silence; then the old chief who had pulled her out of the hand-to-hand fight and brought her back to the palace, went to her and holding her hand, he said: 'Maharaj, you must calm down. You must think again. You are not responsible for the calamity that has befallen the city. You are a fearless woman and you must bear this with fortitude. It is far better to die fighting than die by your own hand. You must now fight your way out of the city. You must leave tonight and break through the enemy's cordon. Go to Kalpi and meet the Peshwa. If in the attempt you die, it will be an honourable death – a far better death than the one you are contemplating.'

The old chief had spoken with the authority of a father speaking to his daughter. Lakshmi Bai felt a great sense of gratitude. She bent down and touched his feet. The old chief spoke again, 'Think of this also, Maharaj. So long as you and your son Damodar are alive and can get to the Peshwa, there is always a chance of retrieving our fortunes so that the *bhagwa jhanda* of the Marathas may yet wave again over Jhansi. Yes, you can fight again; this is not the end of the road.' The Rani with bowed head said, 'I have been a blind fool, Baba. You have shown me the way.'

On the night of 4 April, the Rani made preparations to leave the fort. She assembled members of her household, and bade them farewell. She then showed them the secret passage out of the fort from which they could leave and take refuge. She wore armour with an *angarkha* (tunic) over it and a turban on her head. Carrying a sword and two loaded revolvers in her cummerbund, the Rani rode out of the fort on her favourite white horse. Seated behind her and fastened to her back with a silken sash was her son Damodar. She was escorted by 200 fully-armed selected troops, which included some of her loyal Afghans. Her father, Moropant, was part of her escort. Each of her companions carried gold *mohur*s in a bag tied to their belts.

Lakshmi Bai and her party had not gone far before the enemy pickets were aroused. Her escort was attacked and a skirmish developed. Many of her men were killed and her party got separated as the pickets and her *sowar*s got mixed up. The Rani took advantage of the confusion and evading the enemy, she rode out of the British line. She was followed by a woman companion and two body guards. The four of them and Damodar escaped in the direction of Kalpi. They were followed by some British cavalry who soon gave up the chase as the Rani's horses were swifter and they had not realized the identity of their quarry.

Rose was astounded and dismayed when he discovered that Lakshmi Bai had escaped. Lieutenant Dowker of the Hyderabad cavalry and a body of horsemen were sent after the Rani. He caught up with the Rani at Bhandar where she had stopped for food. She was about to leave when Dowker attacked her. But she was too quick for him. With a powerful stroke of her sword she wounded him severely and he fell into the dust. She would have cut him to pieces but for timely help from one of the cavalrymen. While Dowker was being assisted, the Rani and her three attendants made off.

Lakshmi Bai had always been a splendid rider and her horse was a rare animal. Riding hard, she reached Kalpi, the Peshwa's headquarters, on 5 April, having traversed 163 kilometres of rugged country in twenty-four hours which, in itself, is a formidable task.

As discussed earlier, horrendous atrocities were committed both by the British as well as the Indians in this rebellion. After the fall of Jhansi, it was the turn of the inhabitants of this city to be put through the horror of wholesale slaughter and looting. That night,

Godse looked at the city from the roof-top and the whole of Jhansi looked like a cremation ground with fires blazing everywhere.

Parasnis adds that the main palace that had the accumulated wealth of several generations of Maharajas was denuded of all its treasures, the Panna diamonds and other gems, the priceless carpets and miniature paintings and other artefacts. He says that the greatest loss was the library. These books were irreplaceable and according to Parasnis this wanton destruction by the British was worse than the ancient depredation of the Mongols.

The loot from the palace, the horses and elephants and other treasures, were auctioned by the British. Scindia of Gwalior delightedly snapped up most of the prize animals and other precious items from the palace.

After her incredible twenty-four hour ride from Jhansi, Lakshmi Bai arrived at Kalpi at midnight with her ten-year-old son strapped behind her. Kalpi, north-west of Jhansi and on the bank of river Jumna, was a major rebel stronghold and the headquarters of Rao Saheb, Lakshmi Bai's childhood friend. Rao Saheb had assumed the title of Peshwa at the outbreak of the rebellion and was encamped there with his army.

Their meeting the next morning was an embarrassing one for Rao Saheb. It was only because of the ignominious defeat of his army at Betwa, that Lakshmi Bai had lost her capital and was now a fugitive. Her despair was visible as was her anger. Rani Lakshmi Bai said, 'We have not had adequate support from you.' She then unsheathed her sword and declared, 'Your great ancestors had presented this weapon to us and I will wield it till I die. Give me an army and I will fight the enemy.'

These spirited words uttered by this beautiful and great-hearted woman, who had lost so much, left no one unmoved. Present at this time at Kalpi were Tatya Tope; her old allies Mardan Singh, the Raja of Banpur; the Raja of Shahgarh; and other rebel rajas and several of the Rani's soldiers, including her cavalrymen and her Afghans. The Rani soon saw that the troops at Kalpi were composed of diverse groups who had gathered under one flag and had a common objective. Rani could immediately see that half their numbers were composed of ill-trained peasants and camp followers who were more interested in plunder than actual fighting. She told Rao Saheb that the army was not sustained by strict military discipline and subordination and emphasized the need for much more training. She also pressed Rao Saheb to reorganize the forces.

Sir Hugh Rose, meanwhile, allowed time to his men for rest and recuperation and remained at Jhansi for three weeks. He also appealed to the commander-in-chief for reinforcements and was joined by a second brigade and the 71st Highlanders.

Meanwhile, the governor general offered a reward for the capture of the Rani of Jhansi and the Nawab of Banda, stating that 'the sum offered for the Nawab should not exceed Rs 10,000 and that for the Baee (Rani of Jhansi) should be Rs 20,000.'

At Kalpi, some of the rebel leaders started to resent the respect and importance that was being given to the Rani. The rebel leaders, although bound by a common hatred for the British, were vastly different personalities. Women were in any case, considered lesser beings, and it was unheard of for them to lead armies. Consequently, Rao Saheb was persuaded to appoint Tatya Tope as the commander of the army. He would have been better advised to have appointed the Rani, who had a real flair for leadership.

Nevertheless, the Rani continued to exercise considerable influence in planning. She suggested that the Peshwa's army should go forward 70 kilometres towards Jhansi and meet the enemy on favourable ground at the town of Kunch. This site offered several defensive advantages.

As Rose approached Kunch on 5 May, it was a flank attack that he opted for. He made a flank march with his entire force to the north-west of Kunch. A three-pronged attack by Rose's army followed, with the huge siege guns directing their fire on the town. The flank attack caused the rebels to draw back although, for a time, Major Orr commanding the Hyderabad Contingent was pushed back by a counter attack of musket fire and Maratha swords. But the well-trained Indian *sipahi*s of the British forces forged ahead, despite heavy rebel artillery and musketry fire. The battle was a short one and Tatya's army was completely defeated. The British were, however, unable to capitalize on this victory as they were too exhausted to keep up the pursuit and Tatya Tope's army was able to withdraw to Kalpi.

Tatya fled ahead of his men to Charkhi, a village about 30 kilometres away. From there, he disguised himself and made for Gwalior. His goal was to attempt to win over as many of the well-trained *sipahi*s from the Gwalior army as possible. As he was away at Gwalior, he missed the crucial battle at Kalpi which took place soon after. The Rani, who had participated in the battle, returned to Kalpi with her Jhansi horsemen. She was bitterly disappointed, but was ready to fight on indefinitely and hoped that wiser counsels would prevail in the coming conflict at Kalpi.

The defeat at Kunch led to many recriminations among the Peshwa's army. The infantry sipahis taunted the cavalry for having abandoned them, while the cavalry blamed the gunners. The men of all the three arms accused Tatya Tope of faulty tactics and of having disappeared from Kunch too quickly. The Jhansi cavalry also came in for criticism for being over-solicitous of the Rani in the field of battle and the Afghans were charged with having left the field too soon. The morale of the men had plummeted, but by a stroke of good fortune, the Nawab of Banda arrived at Kalpi at this juncture with 2,000 cavalry and some cannons and infantry. This put a very different complexion on matters and the Nawab's efforts, backed by the energy and confidence of the Rani, changed the mood from despair to confidence. The *sipahi*s who had left Kalpi returned from their hideouts in the villages and forests, and in a few days the army was ready to fight once again.

Kalpi was the last stronghold of the rebels and a major storehouse of ammunition, which they could not afford to lose. Rao Saheb held a council of war at which the Rani pointed out that the extensive ravines around Kalpi were a major feature and their plan must take full advantage of them. A skilful battle plan was then drawn up and the Rani was confident that if it was carried out with courage and resolution, victory would be theirs.

Meanwhile, Rose had also strengthened his army. Colonel Maxwell with the Camel Corps, which was composed mainly of

Sikhs, had been sent to join Rose. The Camel Corps was to play a crucial role in the ensuing battle. Between the British camp and Kalpi, there was an extraordinary labyrinth of ravines over which the movement of artillery and cavalry would be severely restricted, but which provided excellent cover for infantry. Within the ravines, Rao Saheb had constructed trenches and barricades, further strengthening his position. Even if Rao Saheb's troops were driven out of the ravines, they could still fall back on eighty-four temples built of solid masonry. These temples constituted a second line of defense and the town of Kalpi, a third line of defense.

Rose instructed Colonel Maxwell to remain north of the Jumna river, shell Kalpi with his batteries and try to blow up the rebel's powder magazine. Rose kept his main forces south of the river and occupied the ground between the Jumna and the Jalalpur-Kalpi road.

The rebel plan was that they would make an ostentatious display of force and launch a false attack on the British left wing near the Jalalpur road. They then proposed to steal up the ravines with their main body of men and try to overwhelm the British right wing. They hoped that this wing would be weakened because detachments from here would have to be sent to support the British left wing against the false attack. Following up on this plan, the rebels marched out in force at 10 o'clock on 22 May and threatened the British left wing, opening fire with their cannons. This attack, headed by Rao Saheb in person and the Nawab of Banda, though intended only as a feint, became more effective than expected and the British left wing was in trouble.

Rose, however, did not detach any men from the right, as had been expected by the rebels. Since his spies had informed him of the heavy concentration of rebel troops in the ravines to the right.

Suddenly, the whole line of ravines became a mass of fire, the rebel batteries opened up and their infantry, climbing from below, poured overwhelming musketry fire on the right of the British line. The superior British Enfield rifles had become clogged by constant use in all kinds of weather and the men found it difficult to load them. The rebels poured in volleys, which the British replied to only feebly. At this stage, the rebels launched a fierce attack on the enemy's right wing and the Rani led a brilliant charge. At the head of the Red Cavalry of Gwalior, she charged straight into and through the British line. This sudden onslaught unnerved the British soldiers and their Indian comrades and they were forced to retreat so far back that they reached their own guns and mortar emplacements at the rear. The Rani pressed on and got within 20 yards of the British field guns and mortars and outpost tents, and her men sabred the gunners. Another quarter of an hour, and the British would have been massacred.

But Rose, the canny general, had kept the right wing reserve at full strength and not moved any men to support the left wing. When he saw the collapse, he moved swiftly and brought up the Camel Corps and, leading those himself, charged at the advancing rebels. The two sides were locked in close combat but, gradually, the rebel stranglehold was loosened and finally they were pushed back into the ravines. The Sikh sipahis of the Camel Corps had dramatically turned the tide.

Meanwhile, Rao Saheb, fighting on the left, had hoped to send reinforcements to the Rani on the right, but his attack collapsed and he was driven back to Kalpi. The news of his rout shattered all hope of victory for the Rani and when further resistance was pointless, she and her men also returned to Kalpi. Another battle had been lost.

Brigadier Sir John Smythe says:

> In this day's fighting, the rebels had displayed resolution and a tactical sense far above anything they had shown before ... it is certain the Rani not only influenced the planning but was herself well forward in the attack, encouraging and directing the rebel troops. It is said that she herself led the vital charge which so nearly routed Brigadier Stuart in the crucial phase of the battle. If only the other rebel leaders had been of the same calibre as the Rani, who knows what might have happened.

That night the Rani had to sleep under a tree. It was just as well that she did, as one of the shells from the enemy batteries burst in her room at Kalpi and killed two of her attendants.

Kalpi fell the next day. The morale of the rebels had been broken and there was no resistance. The campaign had now been completed and Rose issued a farewell proclamation to his troops, but before he could actually leave, the most shattering news arrived at the headquarters. This news, in the words of a Calcutta newspaper, 'caused throughout India a sensation hardly less than that caused by the news of the outbreak of the mutiny'.

From Kalpi, Rani Lakshmi Bai and Rao Saheb had fled to Gopalpur, 80 kilometres to the south-west of Gwalior. Here they were joined by the Nawab of Banda and Tatya Tope. They had suffered disastrous losses; they had no guns, no equipment and only the remains of an army. They were surrounded by their enemies who were closing in and the morale of their soldiers was poor. Dark clouds of despair hung over them. They wanted to continue fighting but did not know how. The sipahis wanted to go back to Awadh, while Rao Saheb thought their best chance lay in the Deccan, which was once the heartland of the Maratha Empire and where he hoped, once the Peshwa's standard was raised, the other Maratha states would also rise in rebellion. But the Deccan was 1,000 kilometres to the south.

It was then that the Rani pulled them out of the gloom and despondency. She said to them, 'The whole Maratha military tradition has been based on the possession and defence of impregnable fortresses. Shivaji fought the mighty Mughals because he had the strategic forts of Sinhagrah, Raigad and Toran. We just cannot run away, we will be pursued and destroyed. We now need to attack and capture a strong fort and with that as our base; we have to continue our struggle till victory is ours.'

They waited in tense silence for the Rani to continue, 'It is the great fort of Gwalior that I have in mind. If we can capture that and win over the Gwalior army to our cause, we will acquire not only military strength but also political influence. We can start anew, we can fight again. Tatya Tope has already visited Gwalior and done much spade work.'

The assembly was electrified. It was a daring and an original suggestion and could have serious repercussions for the British. When the news reached Calcutta that the Rani and Rao Saheb were on their way to Gwalior, the British were stunned. Gwalior was in some ways the key to India. Lord Canning telegraphed Sir R. Hamilton, 'If Scindia joins the mutiny; I shall have to pack off tomorrow.' The Rani's scheme was accepted and acted upon immediately.

Maharaja Jiyajee Rao Scindia was the most important of the Maratha chiefs. The reasoning at Gwalior was that if they joined the rebellion, the English could be confined to Bengal, but what would happen to Gwalior? There would be many contenders for supremacy, the Mughals, Sikhs, and Nana Saheb. Scindia refused to take those risks and preferred servitude.

The people of Gwalior and the army, however, thought differently. Within living memory, their people, the Marathas, had dominated India, and the Emperor at Delhi was a puppet in their hands. In their eyes, the Maharaja was playing a doubtful role. Rao Saheb and Tatya Tope thought that with all ground work done by Tatya, they would be able to enter Gwalior without firing a shot, but they were mistaken.

Scindia marched out with about 8,000 men and several guns and took up a position about 2 miles east of the rebels at Morar. Scindia's guns opened fire on the Peshwa forces, which was totally unexpected and contrary to Tatya Tope's assurances that Scindia's army would not fight. For a while they thought that the volley was really a salute of welcome, till the shells started falling close. The Rani ridiculed their expectations and their dismay, and at the head of 2,000 cavalry advanced towards the guns. The smoke of the discharge from Scindia's cannons had scarcely disappeared when the 2,000 horsemen led by the Rani charging at a gallop, carried the guns. Immediately after, the rebels raised a loud cry of 'Deen, Deen!' (religion). Scindia's troops responded in the same manner, and fraternized with the Peshwa's army. Many went off to eat watermelons in the bed of the Morar river, which was very sensible considering the searing heat of June.

Scindia then fled from the field and did not draw rein till he reached the safety of Agra. He even left his Rani and his seraglio behind. The first part of the Rani's plan had succeeded admirably. Rao Saheb and his army entered Gwalior in triumph. They took the treasury and Scindia's jewels, the latter said to be of great value. With the money the rebel leaders paid Scindia's army and their own men several months' wages.

With the fall of Gwalior, the Peshwa's army had not only acquired the strong fort of Gwalior but also a well-trained army and about fifty guns. They had fled in a helpless state from Kalpi, leaving all their equipment and stores behind them and losing many of their men, who had dispersed into the countryside. But now they had once more acquired military strength, and equally important, political power. If Rao Saheb could arrange for the defence of Gwalior and then march southward to the Deccan and unfurl the standard of the Peshwas there, the Maratha states, including the powerful Holkar, who were still loyal to their former government, would join the rebellion with disastrous consequences for the British.

Tatya Tope was proclaimed as the Peshwa and Rao Saheb as the Governor of Gwalior. To celebrate the fall of Gwalior, Rao Saheb held a grand durbar. The festivities went on for days, almost as if liberation from the hated British had already been accomplished.

One person was notably absent from the festivities. Rani Lakshmi Bai refused to take part and told Rao Saheb: 'You are wasting time on trivialities and celebrating before victory has been won. If you do not prepare immediately for war, you will destroy our chances. Do not underestimate the strength and resources of the British. They will soon be at Gwalior. They have to hurry because the monsoon is round the corner and the rains will bog down the movement of their guns and equipment. We have no time to lose.'

Tatya Tope also joined the Rani in cautioning Rao Saheb. This had some effect because Rao Saheb took a few constructive steps. Letters were dispatched to rebel rajas still in the district, notably, Raja Mardan Singh of Banpur and the Raja of Shahgarh, both worthy allies of the Rani, to join in the government at Gwalior. The command of the bulk of the troops, encamped outside the city, was entrusted to the Rani of Jhansi. Those within the town took orders from Tatya Tope.

The news of the fall of Gwalior reached Rose on 4 June at Kalpi. Rose immediately realized the full danger of the situation. Gwalior was in the hands of the rebels and the monsoon was imminent, making it impossible to move guns and heavy equipment. It was the least favourable time for military operations.

In north and central India, the British had troops to spare as the revolt had been suppressed in most other parts of the country. Immediate and heavy reinforcements were sent to Rose. Chief among these were the Rajputana Field Force and the Hyderabad Contingent.

A reconnaissance had indicated that the weakest side of Gwalior was towards the east, where the city was commanded by some hills which were out of range of the insurgent's cannons in the fort. This, as it happened, was the sector whose defense had been entrusted to the Rani of Jhansi.

The rebels were completely surprised by the rapidity of Rose's advance from Kalpi. The Rani's strong criticism of her fellow leaders for wasting time in feasting and celebrating was fully borne out. Rao Saheb and others who had been so full of confidence were now in panic and realized that their lack of preparedness was a fatal mistake. They tried to make last minute dispositions of their guns and men. Tatya Tope rushed to see Lakshmi Bai to ask for her advice. He found her furious at the colossal stupidity of her fellow leaders. She said to him, 'The only thing you can do now is to take your troops for one glorious attack on the English without caring for the result. I am ready to do my duty. You do yours. Go ahead and God be with you.'

The Rani knew that this was her last battle. She donned her armour, buckled her jewelled sword and mounted her horse. The very sight of her, thus armed, and mounted and wearing her fabulous necklace of pearls around her neck, gave new heart to her men. Many of them carried this last picture of her in their minds and went into battle. She was an inspiring and beautiful woman and she had fought shoulder to shoulder with these men, sharing their dangers, and their fears in battle. They were willing to die with her and swore solemn oaths that they would fight to the bitter end. Raghunath Singh Nauner and Munder, one of her woman companions, were by her side.

The Rajputana and Hyderabad forces moved forward to Kotah-ki-Serai, about 8 kilometres from Gwalior. Here the Rani ordered her hidden guns to open fire and at the same time charged suddenly from behind the hills. This fierce attack surprised Brigadier Smith and he had to withdraw rapidly, losing heavily in the process. At the same time, a body of the Rani's cavalry threatened the baggage of the British Indian troops. Matters now looked serious for Smith and he had to send back a detachment to defend the baggage and the rear. He dare not advance that day.

The next morning, on 17 June, Smith advanced again and lured the rebel troops from their sheltered positions into the open plain, where his cavalry could operate freely. The Rani advanced to meet them under covering fire from the artillery. The battle raged fast and fierce, but Smith had been reinforced by a squadron of the 8th Hussars under Captain Heneage. Still the rebels held their ground and the Rani led her troops to repeated and fierce attacks, but her ranks were gradually becoming thinner and thinner. She was in the foremost ranks rallying her shattered troops and 'wielding two swords by two hands, holding the reins of the horse in her mouth'. Suddenly she fell from a carbine shot, mortally wounded. The British did not know at what stage of the battle the Rani fell, as she was in cavalry uniform and could not be distinguished from the other soldiers. One of her attendants picked her up and carried her to the rear. Her 200 picked men fought to the last man as they had sworn to her and it was only after their deaths that the Hussars broke through.

The British did not know that the Rani had been killed till two days later. Accounts of her death vary considerably. Some say that she was struck down by a sabre cut; others opine that she was killed by a bullet or a shell. Whatever the truth, she died a death that every true soldier would be proud of, on the battlefield, fighting to the last breath. Thus the Peshwa's army lost their most inspiring and effective leader.

Another version of her death suggests that, although mortally wounded, the Rani was not actually killed on the field, but was carried off the ground, and ordered a funeral pyre to be made, which she ascended and fired with her own hand. Today, a small temple marks the place near Phool Bagh, where the Rani's body was said to have been cremated.

The Rani had always been haunted by the fear that if killed in battle, her body may fall into the hands of the *melicha* foreigners and be defiled by their touch. Her bodyguards, which still included Raghunath Singh Nauner, had this etched on their hearts and in every action they were like her shadow and finally when she did fall they extracted her from the melee and carried her to the rear.

Sir O.T. Burne, who was at one time Military Secretary to the commander-in-chief in India, in his book *Clyde and Strathnairn*, published in 1891, gives another poignant detail about the Rani's last action before her death. 'This Indian Joan of Arc was dressed in a red jacket and trousers and a white turban. She wore Scindia's celebrated pearl necklace, which she had taken from his treasury. As she lay mortally wounded in her tent, she ordered these ornaments to be distributed among her troops. The whole rebel army mourned her loss.'

As soon as it became known that the Rani was dead, the rebels lost heart. There were minor engagements between the British and the rebels and desultory fighting continued for two days, but Gwalior fell to the enemy. The remnants of the Peshwa's army melted away into the countryside.

General Rose in his battle report paid generous tribute to the Rani and compared her to Joan of Arc, a comparison that came naturally to many European observers. He also wrote the sentence that has since become famous, 'The most important result was the death of the Ranee of Jhansi who although a lady, was the bravest and best military leader of the rebels.'

SELECT BIBLIOGRAPHY

Forrest, Sir George, *A History of the Indian Mutiny: Reviewed and Illustrated from Original Documents,* Asian Educational Services, 2006 (Reprint).

Godse, Vishnu, *Ankho Dekha Gadar* (Hindi translation by Amrit Lal Nagar) Vision Rajpal, Delhi, 19198.

Grant, Sir Hope, *Incidents in the Sepoy War 1857-58*, Blackwood, London, 1873.

Gupta, P.C., *Nana Sahib and the Rising at Cawnpore*, Oxford, 1963.

Holmes, Thomas Rice, *A History of the Indian Mutiny and of the Disturbances which Accompanied it among the Civil Population*, Macmillan & Co., London, 1904.

Kaye, Sir John William, *A History of the Sepoy war in India 1857-1858,* W.H. Allen & Co., London, 1880.

Lang, John, *Wandering in India: And other Sketches of Life in Hindustan* Routledge, Warne, & Routledge, London, 1861.

Lowe, Thomas, *Central India During the Rebellion of 1857 and 1858,* Longman, Green, Longman and Roberts, London, 1860.

Malleson, George Bruce, *History of the Indian Mutiny: 1857-1858,* W.H. Allen & Co., London, 1878.

Pal, Dharm, *Tatya Tope: The Hero of India's First War of Independence 1857-1859*, The Hindustan Times, New Delhi, 1955.

Roberts, Fred, *Letters Written During the Indian Mutiny,* Macmillan & Co, London, 1924.

Russell, William Howard, *My Diary in India: 1858-59*, Cambridge University Press, London, 1860.

Savarkar, V.D., *The Indian War of Independence: 1857*, London, 1907.

Sen, S.N., *Eighteen Fifty Seven*, Publications Division, New Delhi, 1958.

Smyth, John George, *The Rebellious Rani,* Frederick Muller London, 1966.

Tahmankar, D.V., *The Rani of Jhansi*, MacGibbon & Kee, London, 1958.